01-16

My Search For

Augusta Pierce Tabor

Leadville's First Lady

My Search For
Augusta Pierce Tabor
Leadville's First Lady

by

Evelyn E. Livingston Furman

Printed in the United States of America
1993
Quality Press
Denver, Colorado

This book is lovingly dedicated
to my daughter
Sharon P. Furman Krueger

Table of Contents

Chapter 1   The Research . . . Pierce Genealogy Found   1

Chapter 2   The Home On Top Of The Hill   9

Chapter 3   Augusta Meets Horace Tabor   29

Chapter 4   Pioneer Life In Deep Creek   32

Chapter 5   The Wedding   35

Chapter 6   Heading West   40

Chapter 7   A Trip To Tabor Valley   46

Chapter 8   From Kansas and Denver
To California Gulch   50

Chapter 9   The New Mining Area   66

Chapter 10   The Little Pittsburgh Discovery   72

Chapter 11   Tabor Luck Prevails   75

Chapter 12   Leadville Grows   86

Chapter 13   The Tabors Build   89

Chapter 14   Evergreen Lakes   97

Chapter 15   Tabor Builds In Denver   110

Chapter 16   Enter Baby Doe - Augusta's Darkest Hour   117

Chapter 17   The Agonies of Augusta - The Divorce   120

Chapter 18   The Senate Race and H.A.W. Tabor's Speech   125

Chapter 19   Another Marriage   132

Chapter 20   Where Is the Luck?   137

Chapter 21	The Truth About Augusta Tabor and The Declining Years	143
Chapter 22	The Death of Augusta Tabor	147
Chapter 23	Augusta's Descendants Located	153
Chapter 24	Research and a Visit With Friends	158
Chapter 25	Research and a Visit With The La forgues	173
Chapter 26	Following the "Silver Star" and Ending the Tabor Dream	181
	The "Silver Star", Poem by Sharon Furman Krueger	185
	Appendix	187

Acknowledgments

My special thanks to my daughter, Sharon P. Furman Krueger, who first typed the original text from my handwritten notes. This IBM (compatible) computerized text was transferred into the Macintosh computer belonging to Eugene F. Todd of Cheyenne, Wyoming, who then proceeded to edit the many revisions of the manuscript thereafter, with great assistance of Eleanor Waggener as the expert typist. Fortunately, Eugene, who holds a graduate degree in history and teaches at the college level, has had a 40-year fascination with the Tabor story of Colorado! I am grateful for his advice and consultations.

I am thankful to Lillian Elizabeth Pierce Braley for introducing me to Horace Howell Pierce and informing me that he had the Pierce genealogy. She was kind in loaning me her book by North, <u>History of Augusta</u>, <u>Maine</u>.

Horace Howell Pierce was especially helpful in giving me a copy of his own genealogy which tied into Augusta's genealogy. This was a great time saver for me, and I am very thankful to Horace Howell Pierce for his invaluable help.

Mike Molloy was instrumental in getting me started on the research in Maine. He furnished me with transportation to all places I needed to go, and he made sure that I had transportation to other locations of interest. He and his family were always available (Tyke, Andrew and Kate.) Mike's assistance was invaluable also in finding people that could assist me in more research. He gave time from his busy schedule to see that my research went successfully.

Andrew Molloy was so good to take pictures that I needed for my book. Mike and Andrew led me to Ernest Richardson.

I am greatly indebted to Ernest Richardson. He took time from his busy schedule to help me locate the William Pierce homestead and the Pierce Quarry. After he introduced me to Bea and John Rebman, and inspecting their deed to their property, the research went along at a fast pace. A trip to the courthouse and tracing the deeds back to the original of William Pierce completed that research. Ernest brought in a genealogist, Lois Thurston, who also helped.

Bea Rebman gave generously of her time to help me. An examination of her deed revealed the needed information to trace to the William Pierce original deed. She kindly furnished me with photographs for the book. I do here express my gratitude to Bea and her family.

I am indebted to Thierry Perrot, that wonderful person that located Augusta's descendants in France. Through him I was soon in touch with

Philippe Laforgue and family. I thank Thierry Perrot for his help, kindness, and valuable assistance.

Marie Helen and Jean Michel Conte were very helpful. Marie Helen also assisted me in locating Philippe Laforgue. The Contes entertained us in their stately mansion. The French food served there was delicious, and they also took us to restaurants where we enjoyed more French cooking. They showed us the sights of Paris and Versailles. We appreciate their generosity, and again I thank them for everything.

Philippe Laforgue and wife Jeanine gave valuable assistance in making their family history collection available, such as scrapbooks, newspaper articles, photographs and other documents. I was delighted with the rare and unpublished photographs of Augusta Pierce Tabor. They furnished transportation everywhere that we needed to go, and gave us the use of an apartment. We thank them for the special dinners at their home and in restaurants of the area. We were well entertained by the Laforgues and were fascinated by the sights of Paris and Versailles. At another special dinner in their home, we were introduced to more members of the Laforgue family and good friends. All of your valuable assistance is greatly appreciated. Thanks again.

I am greatly indebted to Elva and John Pogar and to Iris and Meikle Gardner. They helped me with my research in Vermont. They generously furnished me with transportation to the area where Horace Tabor was born and reared. They also located the original birth place of Horace Tabor--now a sugar house. They took me to the home of the Tabor descendants that owned the Tabor family album. Here I found rare photographs of Augusta Tabor. I am most thankful to Elva for her extra efforts and help in making the research a success.

My thanks to Debbie Jacobs for furnishing me with genealogy of her family, including that of Horace Tabor. She also gave me a photo of the sugar house, birthplace of H.A.W. Tabor.

Many thanks go to a very dear friend, Mildred Viola. She took me numerous times in her car to the State Historical Society and Denver Public Library to do research. She is interested in the Tabor story and especially the Tabor Opera House. She furnished the labor to make velvet drapes for the Tabor Box. Laura Viola has also helped.

My special thanks go to others that helped: Pete Cain, Reginald Page, Stella Turner, Anabel and Richard Parshall, Peggy Ducharme; also Nadine Goodwin, Mrs. Dell Mar Akin, Helen Miller, A.E. Inman, Shirley Fielder, Cindy and Mike Hubbard, and Richard Krueger.

Preface

No person has devoted more energy or years of her lifetime to the preservation of the Tabor legacy than Evelyn Livingston Furman! Not Augusta Tabor, the first wife of Horace Tabor, who died in 1895 on the evening of what would have been her 38th wedding anniversary had she remained married to the silver king of Colorado. Not even the famous Baby Doe, Tabor's second wife, whose frozen body was found in a shack near the famous Matchless Mine of Leadville in 1935, 52 years after her marriage to one of America's richest men.

But Evelyn Livingston Furman has dedicated 59 years of her life to the Tabor story beginning in 1933 when she first arrived in Colorado and personally met and saw the tattered Baby Doe trudging along the streets of Leadville.

In 1934 Evelyn became the young bride of Gordon Furman, a gold miner, who leased and worked the Valley Mine only a couple miles out of Leadville. The newlyweds actually became neighbors to Baby Doe when they honeymooned through their first long Rocky Mountain winter in an isolated mining cabin located in close proximity to the desolate hovel where Baby Doe maintained her vigilant watch over the Matchless Mine in hopes that it would produce millions again to restore the Tabor fortune. Baby Doe had already become a solitary and paranoid recluse who bitterly resisted all intrusions into her private world. However, Baby Doe did appreciate reading old editions of the <u>Denver</u> <u>Post</u> left at her shack by Evelyn's father-in-law.

But this was only the beginning of Evelyn Furman's fascinating involvement with the continuing Tabor saga of Colorado. Her historical interest was climaxed in 1955 with she and her mother's acquisition of the famous Tabor Opera House of Leadville. Evelyn and her mother Mrs. Florence A Hollister, a retired school teacher, began a never-ending project of restoration and preservation of one of Colorado's most celebrated historical landmarks. The prestigious opera house became the first of H.A.W. Tabor's many grandiose showpieces in Colorado, perpetuating the illustrious Tabor name and fame, and all funded with enormous wealth newly acquired from striking the mother-lode of rich silver deposits in his Matchless Mine. His monetary generosity made him not only the founding father of Leadville, but propelled him into the highest echelon of political-financial power brokering within the state of Colorado.

Restoration and management of the Tabor Opera House, making it one of Leadville's top tourist attractions, would be time consuming enough for any other public-minded citizen. But not for Evelyn Furman! She authored two books dealing again the continuing saga of the Tabor story in Colorado: Silver Dollar Tabor, (1982) about the tragic life of Tabor's youngest daughter, Silver Dollar, born to Horace and Baby Doe; and The Tabor Opera House (1972).

In her book Silver Dollar Tabor, Evelyn successfully challenges the *historical myth* perpetuated by Caroline Bancroft in her booklet Silver Queen that all contact between Baby Doe with both her daughters had been severed during their later years. Granted, their family relationship was estranged, and neither Lily nor Silver ever returned to Colorado to visit their mother once they left the state as young women, but there was occasional correspondence as evidenced by the letters which Evelyn included in her book.

Now Evelyn Furman has done it again! With this volume she tells the heartwarming and heartbreaking story of Augusta Tabor; Horace's first wife and, indeed, one of the leading pioneer women of Colorado.

The author contends how unfairly the Tabor legend has treated Augusta by comparing photographs of her as the elder Mrs. Tabor, taken in her 60's; to glamorous photographs of the beautiful Lizzy McCourt Doe, better known as Baby Doe, the second and much younger wife of U.S. Sen. Horace Tabor.

To prove her point, Evelyn includes a voluminous collection of original Tabor photos, some of which are being printed here for the first time. They visually demonstrate that the younger Augusta Tabor was not only a very attractive lady of considerable feminine charm and beauty in her own right, but also a mature woman of great strength, moral character and pioneer perseverance.

For another comparison, one needs only to compare the photos of Augusta taken in her 60's to those of Baby Doe taken in her later years! Augusta's portrait makes her appear austere and cold, perhaps haughty with her pince-nez glasses, in all her New England countenance. But she was not the straight-laced Victorian in her personal views that she is purported to have been. Had this been true, she would not have been the primary benefactor toward building a Unitarian Church in Denver, and a sincere philosophical believer in the liberal theological thinking traditionally associated with this denomination on all moral and social issues.

The comparison between the first and second wives of H.A.W. Tabor, Augusta and Baby Doe, becomes most apparent when it comes to the respective roles each of them played regarding the monumental Tabor fortune. The prominent role Augusta played in its original acquisition and frugal conservation. And the prominent role Baby Doe played in its frivolous disposition and eventual demise!

It's time for the truth be known about the real Augusta Tabor. And Evelyn Furman is determined to bring us not only the whole historical truth, but new insights into the full dimension of this unique pioneer woman's personal life; as well as her distinguished contribution to Colorado history.

I first became acquainted with Evelyn Furman during one of my many historical treks among the mining towns of Colorado's glorious Rocky Mountains. Even though I was born and raised on my father's cattle ranch along the front range of the Big Horns in northern Wyoming, I attended the University of Denver and did three years of graduate study in Colorado. I have lived in Cheyenne, Wyoming for nearly 30 years but spend a lot of my extra time in the archives of the Colorado Historical Museum and visiting historical sites in the state.

While a student at the DU, over 40 years ago, I first stumbled across the Tabor story and have been enchanted with its drama and trauma ever since. The old Windsor Hotel was still in operation then, although badly deteriorating, and I visited the suites where the Tabors lived (Horace and second wife Baby Doe) during the heyday of their wealth and glory in the early 1880's, and the suite where Sen. Tabor died, broken and penniless, in 1899. (Although as a political sop he was appointed postmaster in Denver one year before his death.)

In Leadville, I visited the restored weather-beaten shack, formerly a tool shed, in which Baby Doe lived the remainder of her life maintaining her lonely and delusional vigilance over the Matchless Mine until her death in 1935. I even returned to the site one evening alone and sat on the bench outside her cabin almost as if awaiting her ghostly visitation. She didn't appear, but I felt myself haunted by unknown spirits of the distant past in the quiet mountain stillness and chill of the evening breeze. My historical sense kept asking the question: What must it have been like for Baby Doe with her memories of former grandeur, as she lived out the final years of her desperate life here in this desolate place, amid the abject poverty that plagued her, and bitter family tragedy and estrangement that burdened her down?

Not many people shared my fascination with the Tabor saga until I met my match in the person of Evelyn Livingston Furman in Leadville! This remarkable woman has lived and walked the Tabor story longer than either the courageous Augusta, Horace's first wife, or Baby Doe, his glamorous second wife.

As a matter of fact, Evelyn Furman embodies characteristics of both the Tabor women in the person of herself. Like Augusta, Evelyn has persevered against overwhelming odds in becoming a respected business woman in Leadville and owner of the famed Tabor Opera House. Like Baby Doe, she maintains her protective vigilance over the opera house as if it were the Matchless Mine. Unlike Baby Doe, however, Evelyn graciously invites visitors to the opera house and welcomes their questions. Like both of Horace's devoted wives, she is dedicated to the preservation of the Tabor legacy.

I offered to proofread and review the first manuscript of this book on Augusta Tabor as written by Evelyn Furman. This resulted in my being a guest in her lovely Leadville home, which in itself is something to behold. It was built in the 1890's right on the main drag of Leadville, which is called Harrison Avenue, just a few blocks up from the Tabor Opera House located along the same street. Its stained glass windows and exquisite parquet wooden floors compliments her priceless collection of beautiful antique furniture which grace every room on both floors.

In her spacious writing room, on the second floor, is Evelyn's handsome desk where she works on her manuscripts. The windows look out upon the historic ole' mining town of Leadville, its streets winding around the slag heaps and up the steep mountain side, all of which figured so prominently in the Tabor story. To the west of town are the lofty summits of Mt. Massive and Mt. Elbert, highest peaks of the Colorado Rockies, majestic and snow capped, even in July, which appear much closer than what they really are because of the shimmering rare atmosphere of the high altitude.

Later, Evelyn was a most gracious guest in our home in Cheyenne where we typed the manuscript into my Macintosh computer and began our several revisions. Always, I insisted that she tell the Augusta Tabor story in her own words, preserving her own literary style and personal expressions of thought and sentiment. Historically, I felt this to be as important as if Augusta or Baby Doe had been asked to write their own story. When writing the biography of an historic personage, newspaper clippings are important for reference and local color, and Evelyn had collected many of these, but I kept encouraging her to tell the story in her own unique way and not allow a reporter to write the story for her. The reason for this was, Evelyn Furman had lived with the Tabor story for nearly 60 years. She knew Augusta Tabor more intimately than any other human being alive today, and the reader deserved to hear Augusta's story from the heart and mind of Evelyn Furman who loved and admired her the most!

I am happy to have been associated, in a very minor way, with this book dealing with the search of Evelyn Furman for the real Augusta

Tabor. Her search led to Augusta's ancestral roots embedded deeply in the granite quarries of New England, and on to modern France where the only direct descendants of Horace and Augusta Tabor are living today.

Beyond my brief association with her authorship of the book, however, was the rare privilege of mine to have made the personal acquaintance of Evelyn Livingston Furman! Every tourist should make it a special point to visit the Tabor Opera House in Leadville just to meet her.

Eugene F. Todd

Evelyn Livingston Furman with Eugene F. Todd in front of the author's historic Leadville home. The ore bucket was used not only to raise raw ore to the surface for processing into bullion, but to transport miners to the lower depths of the gold and silver mines of Colorado.

Elizabeth McCourt Doe Tabor (Baby Doe), second wife of Horace A.W. Tabor. A fair comparison of both wives when they were about the same age. Photo courtesy of the Denver Public Library Western Collection.

Found at last -- the YOUNG Augusta Pierce Tabor -- first wife of HAW Tabor. Photo courtesy of the Amon Carter Museum, Fort Worth, Texas.

Augusta, first wife of Horace Tabor -- from the family picture album owned by Reginald Page of Holland, Vermont. Mr. Page is the son of Harry Page, who married Sadie Tabor, daughter of Lemuel Tabor, a brother of Horace Tabor. This rare photo of Augusta, as a young lady, was discovered in 1985 by the author while doing research in Vermont.

Chapter One
The Research . . . Pierce Genealogy Found

"Well, I can see now why Tabor divorced Augusta and married Baby Doe!" exclaimed a tourist on the Tabor Opera House Tour. Three individual photographs were displayed on the wall of the theater: Augusta, Horace in the center of the arrangement, and Baby Doe on the opposite side. The glamorous Baby Doe, much younger, appeals to the average visitor. Many times, over the years, I have heard this comment from those on tour , "Yes, I can see why Tabor divorced Augusta."

As we all stood gazing at the photographs, I came to the defense of Augusta. "But," I protested, "this was Augusta when older. She, as Horace's first wife, was also beautiful when young."

When Baby Doe first met Horace she was 29 and he was 53; Augusta was about 50. Is it fair to compare women of that age difference?

At the beginning of this writing it seemed that no photographs of Augusta, when a young woman, had been found. Thus, the general opinion prevailed that Augusta was a stern, straight-laced New Englander. I am determined to find a photograph of Augusta, the young and beautiful lady, looking as she did when she married Horace. Surely one such photograph exists somewhere!

Beauty is not the only attribute to be considered. What shall also be emphasized is Augusta's contribution to the early-day history of Colorado. As we shall see, happiness did not always prevail in the life of Augusta. Even the good times were punctuated with continual hardships.

Augusta and Horace Tabor have gone down in history as prominent pioneers in settling and developing The American West. No one has done more for the early development in the Colorado cities of Leadville and Denver than the Tabors. Tabor money has done much for various parts of Colorado and other locations, far and wide.

Augusta has not received the recognition she so deserves. This disturbs me. Therefore, the purpose of this book is not only to give her the credit she deserves, but to bring to the reader new-found information

1

to add to the old. Unpublished photographs are included and the account of my research.

The story of the Tabors never ceases to fascinate me. I came to Leadville in 1933, just for the summer, and never left. Being fascinated with the Tabor story, I did research in Leadville and Denver. I interviewed older people that I met when I first arrived. My search for Tabor history has been a never -ending one. My interest led me to further locations where I might trace the Tabor family to Holland, Vermont; Tabor Valley and Zeandale, Kansas; Oshkosh, Wisconsin; Paris and Versailles, France.

Still to be researched was Augusta, Maine where Augusta was born and grew to womanhood. I was determined to go there and find the information not yet written on the pages of Tabor history. A search through the vital records of Augusta, Maine reveals the names of Augusta, her parents, brothers and sisters. An author, Helen Miller, gave me copies of this information in 1980. She was also interested in Augusta.

Now, for a start with the research, I have information from the vital records of Augusta, Maine to the year 1892, Vol. 1. Under births is disclosed: Louisa Augusta Pierce, daughter of William Babcock Pierce and Lucy S. Pierce, March 29, 1833. Augusta did not use her name Louisa, but was called Augusta. (She was named after the capitol of her native state of Maine.)

Through the years, my curiosity continued to be aroused. Questions in my mind were: Who were the first Pierce ancestors in America, and what is the rest of the genealogy leading to Augusta and her family? Where is the Pierce homestead and the stone quarry? What about Augusta's early life in Maine? Who will take the time to really locate this history missing from the books already written about the Tabors? I set out to find this information and bring it to the forefront.

First, I was determined to locate the early home of Augusta, the William B. Pierce homestead and stone quarry.

All I had to go on concerning the Pierce homestead and quarry was found in an old newspaper clipping with no date. The article reads as follows: " . . . up Church Hill Road on the east side of the river . . . up the winding hill to Pierce's quarries. The Pierce family lived in the house on top of the hill. The granite quarry has never gone out of their possession, and to this day bears the Pierce name." This mystery must be solved. Indeed it is a challenge! I was so excited about a trip to Maine, I could hardly wait to get there. No one knew where the Pierce homestead was, not even those living in Augusta, Maine. No one on Church Hill Road knew where the homestead was located!

2

A phone call to Hallowell, Maine, put me in touch with Mike Molloy. Hallowell is only a few miles from the city of Augusta. Both were once just one city, but later separated into two cities. Mike and I met several years ago when he took the Tabor Opera House tour. He came to Leadville to see where the Tabors made millions in mining. Being interested in all of the Tabor history, he wanted to see the famous Tabor Opera House. The construction of this three-story brick building was the first great accomplishment of the Tabors after they struck it rich.

He remained after the tour, and we discussed many things about the Tabors. He told me then that he would like to help me do the research in Maine. I was impressed with his offer and willingness to help me. Now we were both ready for action. Filled with enthusiasm, Mike called back, telling me about his plans for research. He had located a Pierce home on Church Hill Road, on the outskirts of Augusta. As soon as I arrived he would take me there.

I recall that beautiful autumn day in October 1987 when the plane set down at the airport in Portland, Maine. As I stepped away from the plane, crisp fresh air filled my lungs. It was so invigorating I thought. What a brilliant, blue sky and what a wonderful day! This was not a large city and no pollution here. Filled with energy, I felt anxious to start this new adventure. What a great time to be in New England. Autumn with its beautiful foliage was all about me, and how peaceful it all was.

Mike had made arrangements for his son Andrew to meet me at the airport in Portland. In no time he was by my side and said, "I just knew you must be the one." Here I was, bag and baggage, in Portland, the largest city in Maine. Soon we were on our way to Augusta. I would have the opportunity to see Portland later. It was a beautiful drive. Wide areas on each side of the highway were mowed and well kept; no litter or billboards were to be seen.

As I looked from side to side along the roadway, it seemed like a fairyland of brilliant, fall colors. I was delighted with all I saw and could not hold back my exclamations of joy, seeing autumn in New England! I was impressed by the thick growth of such a variety of trees and bushes. I was soon to learn more of the highways from Mike. He later said, "You know Highway 1 was the first in the United States. It follows the coast of Maine down into the southern states." The Maine Turnpike runs one hundred miles between York and Augusta. U.S. Interstate Highway 95 extends the turnpike from Augusta to Houlton, near the Canadian border. I was impressed by this good highway system.

I was interested in learning about Andrew. He told me, as we traveled along, that he worked for the Kennebec Journal newspaper. I was soon to learn about and see the Kennebec River that runs through Augusta.

3

"I am a photographer," said Andrew. "I would be glad to take any pictures that you want for your book," he added. "How wonderful!" I exclaimed. This was surely a delightful surprise, and I needed many pictures. Andrew is a very likable and capable young fellow. How fortunate to meet a photographer!

Everything seemed to be falling in place!

Soon we were in the city of Augusta; I was so thrilled to set foot on the soil here. "Just think," I said, "the very city where Augusta Pierce was born and raised." As previously mentioned, she was named for the capital of her native state. The capitol building towered over all the other buildings of the city. "Oh, Andrew," I exclaimed, "there's the capitol, I need a picture of it, and all of Augusta that you can capture in that camera of yours."

Mike had reserved a room for me in a good motel with a restaurant attached. How convenient that was for me. Soon I was checked in, and my baggage put in my room. Now we were leaving Augusta, and off to the Mike Molloy home in Hallowell. Once we were inside the door, I noted what a jolly atmosphere prevailed. At last I met Mike's wife, Tyke. Family and friends were also gathered there. Everyone was seated at a large table, and I was invited to join them. This was a fine welcome from all, and I thought what a lively and friendly group filled with fun. I felt very welcome as I sat there enjoying conversation and a refreshing beverage. After the busy days of research that followed, occasionally I was invited to dine with the Molloy family. The entire family went "all out" to make it a gala occasion.

The table was set with beautiful china and silver. I admired the centerpiece and lighted candles which were arranged in good taste. As I took my place at the table, I looked around at all those happy faces and thought to myself, aren't they wonderful! Tyke is a good cook and manages the household so capably. The food was excellent and beautifully prepared. All was served to perfection.

Included in this large Molloy family is an exchange student from Switzerland named Esther. She is about the same age as Kate, one of the Molloy daughters. After dinner, Mike gave me a tour of their home. I was very interested in their beautiful paintings, furniture, books, and other possessions.

Now, back to research plans. I listened attentively as Mike announced , "Tomorrow morning we shall go to Church Hill Road and see this lady I told you about. She is a Pierce, and her name is Lillian Elizabeth Pierce Braley, known as Bette." He had made the appointment

Bette Pierce Braley, by the side of her home at Church Hill Road and South Belfast Road, Augusta, Maine. Photo by Evelyn Furman, 1987.

Horace H. Pierce, Augusta, Maine. Photo courtesy of Horace H. Pierce.

5

Mike Molloy in Portland, Maine -- Helping the author with her research. Photo by Evelyn Furman.

Corner of Church Hill Road and South Belfast Road, Augusta, Maine, 1987. Photo by Andrew Molloy.

to meet with her at the old homestead where she lived with her brother. Horace Hampton Pierce settled here previously, and his son, Walter Sherman Pierce, was next in ownership and also father of Bette (Lillian Elizabeth). Bette was a teacher, who Mike remembers when she taught at Ella Hutchkins Junior High School, about 1960. Mike also taught there at that time, and I was glad Mike had this connection. I could hardly wait for morning and what the day would bring forth. Could this be the Pierce homestead I was searching for? If so, this discovery of the location of Augusta's family home would be solved . . . so . . .

"Everything seemed to be falling into place."

The next morning found us at the corner of South Belfast Road and Church Hill Road, only a short drive from downtown Augusta. "There is the house," said Mike. I was thrilled to see the sign Church Hill Road.

"I must have a picture of that sign on the road," I said. Lillian Elizabeth (Bette) had agreed to share the Pierce history with me, and I was most anxious about that.

On our visit with her, she promptly brought out a very thick book to show me, entitled History of Augusta, Maine by North. This is a record of our first Pierce to settle in America. "Let me show you page four right now," she said. It reads as follows: "The first patent granted by the Council of Plymouth of land in New England was to John Pierce of London and his associates, dated June 1, 1621. This was a roaming patent granting one hundred acres for each settler already transplanted and such as should be transported; the land to be selected by them under certain restrictions. Pierce located at Broad Bay, and afterwards found Brown at New Harbor, with an Indian deed of the territory and they joined their titles and continued the settlement already begun at New Harbor and Pemaquid, which became prosperous and populous as the extensive remains at those points strongly indicate." She closed the book and handed it to me saying, "You may borrow this book if you wish."

How nice that she trusted me with her book. I was glad to have this information. Now, I knew where and how the Pierce history began in this country!

Bette told me about her cousin, Horace Howell Pierce. "He has the complete Pierce history," she said. She made arrangements for me to see him the following day.

"Everything was falling into place."

We were all seated at her table. "Would you like some coffee?" asked Bette. We thought that would be nice, and she made the coffee.

She had the thickest cream that there ever was, and the coffee was delicious. Mike had stopped on the way to buy some doughnuts --- the best I have ever eaten. I was wishing I could find some as good back in Colorado.

Next, we went from the house to the huge barn nearby. How lucky that it was still standing, as so many have been torn down. Standing on the higher ground, I could look over the land Bette pointed out as belonging to the homestead. I was busy with my camera, trying to get pictures of all I saw of interest. (Andrew came out another day, and took pictures in black and white of all I wanted for my book.)

In 1775, Benedict Arnold led an American army through the Kennebec Valley into Canada to attack Quebec. They tried to capture Quebec from the British, but were pushed back.

As we stood looking over the Horace Pierce homestead, Bette pointed to the spot where a huge rock once stood. In 1912 it was moved to Augusta and remains in the present location overlooking the river. It serves as a monument to this event of long ago and marks the spot where the March began. Bette joined Mike and me and directed us to the Wall Cemetery where she showed us the graves of her family. (See Appendix C for descriptions of gravestones.)

At lunch time, we all ate seafood of our choice. (Clam, lobsters, ocean perch, and shrimp are all on the menu in Maine where seafood is a specialty.)

The next day Bette introduced me to her cousin Horace Howell Pierce. His mother named him Howell after her side of the family. He drove Bette and me in his car to the library where we looked over books on Pierce genealogy.

At this point comes the highlight of the search for Pierce genealogy!

Horace gave me a copy of his Pierce genealogy! I tucked it away in my briefcase. Returning to my room later, I read and studied it carefully. Lo and behold, this valuable genealogy included Augusta's family! There it was, right before my very eyes, the William B. Pierce branch, found at last! I was so excited when I came to that name, and how happy I was to have the search of the Pierce history now completed! How wonderful that Horace and his family had taken time to research and preserve their branch of the Pierce history. I am very grateful to Horace Howell Pierce!

Chapter Two
The Home On Top Of The Hill

All was going well, but I still hadn't found the William B. Pierce homestead (parents of Augusta Pierce). That meant I must keep looking. I had come to Augusta, Maine, to search for this home and must locate it. Another day Mike and Andrew drove me up and down Church Hill Road again. Over and over in my mind went the thought of the Pierce home "on top of the hill." (The words from a newspaper clipping.) Perhaps we had not reached the summit, so we checked again. Next stop was the Harvey and Mickie Versteeg place. Mr. Versteeg was an architect. They were friendly and tried to help us saying that they would get their deed from their safety deposit box, and we could then check the ownership down through the years."

We drove on still looking. I scanned the area with great anxiety. I looked eagerly at each house as we drove slowly by. Could this be the "house on the hill?" Driving along Church Hill Road, we came to another home that looked like it might be considered as being "on top of the hill." Like many of these homesteads, it had the original stone foundation.

"Let's stop here," I suggested. After introducing ourselves and stating our mission, we were invited in. This owner was Ernest M. Richardson, a friendly, likable man. He wanted to be helpful, but didn't think a William Pierce ever owned this property. We would check the deed to learn about the past ownerships. He was experienced in tracing property information through deeds. In fact, he said he was then checking his own property. He told us about his house, and how he had purchased it with an acre of ground from the owner, Stella Turner. He related the ownership prior to this, so it seemed, with the information he already had, that no Pierce had lived here. Ernest had restored the interior of his home. He showed us the old well near the house, no longer in use. It was covered with a large, heavy, flat block of stone. We all became interested in the date carved into the block . . . 1847. Andrew took pictures of it. This was an excellent example of the first wells in this area.

Stella Turner and Andrew Molloy. Photo by Joe Phelan, 1987.

Birthplace of Augusta Pierce. William B. Pierce homestead, Augusta, Maine, when owned by Bea and John Rebmann. Photo courtesy of Bea Rebmann, 1987.

Ernest was semi-retired from his position as State Chemist. "I have more time now to do extra things," he said. At present he was busy with work that must be finished before winter set in. Therefore, I felt he would not have much time to help me in my search. He did agree to help me though, and I felt very fortunate in having his assistance in searching for the William B. Pierce homestead, "the house on the hill!"

Everything was falling into place!

"Stella Turner lives over there," said Ernest, pointing to a new home near his own. He knew her well. "Let's go over and visit her," suggested Ernest. "She might have information you need." (Ernest had been telling me about her.) She was a widow, 72 years of age. We knocked on her door, and she invited us in. She was a friendly little lady. Mike, during our conversation, discovered that he had known her daughter years ago when they were both in school.

"She was the smartest person in the class," said Mike, as he chatted with Mrs. Turner about those memories. Mrs. Turner was very gracious, and we sat down to visit with her. Perhaps she might know something about the Pierce history. She brought out her picture album. I found some pictures of the barn and other attached buildings. She offered to let me have copies of any pictures I wanted. I found an old newspaper article that had been cut out and tucked away between the pages of the album.

I was delighted to find it was concerning something we had already heard about several days before. "Oh look here," I exclaimed, "this article concerns the rock Bette told us about, the one that was on their farm." It reads as follows: "Ernest Cunningham, now 84, visited the Fort Western plaque rock the other day and recalled what a job it was to get it there. Cunningham farmed around Augusta most of his adult life and now . . . lives on Church Hill Road. When he saw the KJ story last week of Benedict Arnold's 1775 march to Quebec, it triggered his memory of that big rock. It was 1912, he remembered, when the city hired four men and three teams to move the boulder from the Horace Pierce farm on South Belfast Avenue to its present location opposite the E. E. Taylor Shoe Co. on the bluff overlooking the river. The other men were Daniel Hewins, Wallace Shaw, and George Pierce. Only Cunningham is still alive.

"We loaded the stone with skids onto a wagon, and it took six horses to move it," the spry oldster remembered. Later, a bronze plaque was set into the stone and lettering reads, in part, "an expedition under Col.

Benedict Arnold for capture of Quebec marched from this place in September 1775."

During our conversation with Mrs. Turner, she mentioned an old cemetery on Blair Road. She thought we might find some information on the old tombstones that would be of interest. She agreed to go there with us. "I haven't been there since a young girl, and I'm not sure I can even find it," she said.

I was in favor of this venture and excited about the possibility of finding the Pierce name on a tombstone. In no time, we were all in Ernest Richardson's truck, ready for the search. Mrs. Turner remembered that it was an old road leading off Church Hill Road that we must locate.

After a time, a decision was made as to where this turn off might be. It was a narrow little road that almost went straight down hill. There was a thick growth of trees and underbrush on both sides of the road. The cemetery could never be sighted through all this. We must go on foot and look carefully through the thicket. The ground was wet from a recent rain; water still remained on the leaves of the trees and bushes. There were so many trees, I could hardly squeeze through anywhere.

We all spread out in different directions. "It's on the right side of the road, and there was a vault here," said Mrs. Turner. I thought this was exciting and said, "This is just great!" As I looked back of me, I decided I wasn't making much progress at the low speed I managed. I held back tree branches, but when I released them, they snapped back, spraying me with water. My shoes were getting wet, but I did not mind.

My interest in this exploration was mounting by the minute! I found this new experience great fun, and I was determined to find that cemetery.

The men decided to split their way, with one going back the way we came and the other in the opposite direction. Now they could comb the area thoroughly. After a time, someone shouted "I've found it!" We all made our way to the spot, where most of the gravestones were lying on the ground or toppled over. They were thin stones and many were broken. We were each thrilled over what we found, often reading aloud the inscriptions for the rest to hear.

"Come over here and see this," said one.

"Look at the one I found," I exclaimed. Some of the stones were so weather beaten that the engraving was not legible. There were not so many trees now, so walking was easier.

"Here's the vault," said Mrs. Turner. It was quite large and in fair condition. Mrs. Turner said, " I used to walk along this road when I was young, and sit out here."

"I'm so glad you told us about all this, and I shall never forget this venture," I said. I searched diligently for a marker that might have the name Pierce, but found none. The strange part about this cemetery was that there were so few gravestones. We were told later that many had been stolen. Some of the stones I examined had designs at the top of drooping, weeping willow branches. I was informed that this design of branches meant death.

I found the name Church. Rufus Church died in 1823. I was also told that there were many families by the name of Church once living on Church Hill Road. Could it be possible that this road may have been named for the Church families? Another name was Mc Donald, and it also had the weeping willow design at the top of the stone. Finally, satisfied that we had seen all there was in the cemetery, we worked our way back to the road. Ernest's' truck was left in an open clearing near a field. Looking up the way we had come, we saw people walking down the road in our direction.

"Who could that be in this deserted place?" asked one of our group. Rather spooky, I thought. As they came closer, we could see it was a group of four. Ernest said he knew the people, a man, his wife, and two daughters. They lived farther out on Church Hill Road. After I had been introduced to the newcomers, they were interested in learning about my search for the William Pierce homestead.

The lady said, "Oh, I think we live in that house." I couldn't believe that I had stumbled upon anything this interesting. "We were remodeling the interior, and a letter fell out of the ceiling," she continued. "It was from a Pierce that must have lived in the house," she exclaimed. I was astonished!

"My goodness, how unusual," I said, getting more interested every minute. "Do you still have the letter?" I asked.

"Oh yes, I think so. I put it in my cook book," she replied. She promised to show it to me the next day. How exciting, I thought. When I read the letter I was disappointed, as it was not from Augusta's immediate family. The letter was written by Andrew Newell Pierce and addressed to his father, D.N. Pierce, Leadville, Colorado. It could be relatives of Augusta . . . I would investigate this later.

After the Tabor wealth was established in Colorado, including Leadville, Denver, and the surrounding area, relatives came from the east to seek their fortune in the newly-found Eldorado of Colorado. The Pierces were among the early arrivals.

Evidently, D. N. Pierce saved this letter that he received while working in Leadville, Colorado. When he later returned to his home in Augusta, Maine, he obviously had saved old letters and kept them with his possessions. It may be that this particular letter slipped through an upstairs floor board. Here it remained, preserved for years, until remodeling began --- and it fell out of the ceiling! It was great that I met the family owning that house, and that they had saved the letter. How interesting that this letter should turn up years later in such an unusual place!

Copy of letter that fell out of ceiling:

> *Augusta, Maine, Sept. 2-18-*
> *Dear Father,*
> *Your letter came to hand all right with the ten dollars. Very glad of it. You did not say anything about your feet in your last letter. I wish you would write about it. How are you getting along? We have had a week of awful hot weather ninety-two in the shade. Capt. Springer is dead. Fowler is dying. Old Joe Deniston is dead.*
> *Look for another package we think you had better change your clothes clear through. Write often and take care of yourself.*
> *I have not time to write any more. Will write soon.*
> *From your son,*
> *Andrew Newell Pierce*
> *Envelope address to D.N. Pierce, Leadville, Colorado. Postmarked Sept. 3, 18 ? (blurred) from Augusta, Me., 3-cent stamp*

In the same envelope another letter with the salutation:

> *My Dear Andrew has left a space and I will write a word here . . . we are calculating to come in the fall Andrew and I with Ruth to spend August to May 18 . . . 79 the winter anyway if no longer.*
> *from yours truly*
> *AN Pierce*

Judging from this paragraph, the letters were written in 1878.

Ernest introduced me to another interesting friend of his. She was Lois Thurston, a genealogist. One morning we met at the State Archives. Here, she and Ernest spent time checking over Pierce family records on microfilm. I was so fortunate in having so much help. We investigated vital records of Augusta at Maine State Archives, Library and Museum. I copied census records, library cemetery records, and information from more books on genealogy. I continue to keep a record of all Pierce families I can find.

We still hadn't located the real William B. Pierce homestead. Where was this "house on the hill?" Faithful Ernest was still searching, and he made arrangements for us to meet another family he knew on Church Hill Road. This was the home of Bea and John Rebmann. At the appointed time, we arrived at their home. As we turned into their driveway I noticed the name Rebmann on their mailbox. Once again, I am filled with anticipation and excitement. I looked over the lay of the land and observed that the front yard was level and attractive. In the rear of the house the ground sloped downward to the river below. From this lower level, it appeared that the house was "on the hill." All the places we had checked were on that long, high ridge called Church Hill Road, and "on the hill!"

Bea Rebmann, a lovely lady, responded to our knock on the front door. With a friendly greeting, she invited us in. This must be the right place at last. After introductions, she said, "I have our deed to the house here for you to see."

"Wonderful!" I exclaimed. She led us back through several more rooms to the dining area. We sat there at her table looking over the deed.

Now, we had the information we were seeking. I felt we were making progress in the right direction. This document revealed that the Rebmanns had purchased the house in 1980 from Yveete Sirois. With the information here, we could proceed with the search.

Ernest said, "We will go to the courthouse in the morning and examine the records." Glory be!

I am very grateful to Bea Rebmann for her help in letting us examine her deed. This made it possible to trace ownership of the property back through the years . . . step by step.

Everything was falling into place!

"Come," said Bea, "and let me show you the house." I had quickly surveyed the interior as we walked through. Now, we could take time to see it all at a slower pace. Bea informed us that the windows and doors were new, and they had remodeled parts of the house.

Entering through the front door, one first sees the attractive open stairway. It looked so inviting as I glanced up to the second-floor landing. An uncanny feeling came over me as we stepped into this home . . . almost assuring me that this was Augusta's old home. I imagined I could see Augusta, as a young girl, hurrying up those steps. I commented on the beautiful wood in the balustrade.

Bea said, "Yes we just recently installed the carpeting." In the process of remodeling, I was happy to see that they had incorporated some of the old with the new. Bea has a knack of arranging old and antique items in a pleasing way. All through the house one sees this clever talent put to use. "Here is the living room," said Bea as we stepped into the old front parlor.

"It is lovely," I said. "Is there a fireplace?" I asked.

"Only one," she answered. "The chimney is in that wall behind the clock," she added. (There were four good chimneys originally extending from the cellar to the roof.) She explained more about the chimneys: "A former owner had a new roof installed. At that time two, including the one in the fireplace, were cut off at the roof line. The remaining two are operable. One chimney is used for the wood burning stove in the kitchen and the other chimney is used in connection with the oil burning stove."

"Oh, look at the ceiling!" I exclaimed. I was overjoyed upon learning that the original tin, or metal ceiling, remains and is still used. It looks to be in perfect condition, but painted.

Bea led us on through the house to the large kitchen. "What a nice large kitchen" I commented. The old, original potato bin has been removed from the cellar and made into a breakfast bar, where it occupies a prominent place in the room. The kitchen today is interesting and is unique with Bea's clever arrangements. New plumbing in the house was a necessary convenience.

I liked the huge, long pantry just off the kitchen. Just think of all the shelves that once lined the walls. No doubt there was a hand coffee grinder attached to the wall somewhere.

Bea now uses this pantry area for storage for her puppetry articles, dolls, and supplies. She gives puppet shows for schools, libraries, churches, public and private groups. She calls this her Honeycomb Theater. In addition to this, she keeps busy with her family responsibilities and attends a class in photography. She volunteered to take pictures for me of anything I wanted for this book. How fortunate I am to have all this help! One of her young sons is interesting to talk with also. He likes history and antiques and showed me interesting items.

Here we are in the dining area. All through the house the furniture is new and comfortable. I felt Augusta had walked over these floors, just as I was doing now. I'm, perhaps, sitting in rooms where she spent time sewing, mending, and helping her mother with household chores.

The upstairs bedrooms were modernized and beautifully done, as were the bathrooms. Skylights were installed, and all was light and attractive. Again, Bea had added her own personal touches with old and interesting antique pieces. It was necessary to rewire the house. Bea told us that when they moved into the house there was only one electric light on the second floor, and it was at the top of the stairs. All wiring was old and only the one bare bulb in use.

I was delighted with the original wide floor boards here, which were all nicely finished. Just think how Augusta and all the family walked over these very boards many times!

William B. Pierce home when owned by Bea and John Rebman, Christmas, 1987. Photo courtesy of Bea Rebmann.

Interior of the William B. Pierce home when owned by Bea and John Rebmann. Front hallway and stairs. Augusta tripped up and down these steps many times. Photo courtesy of Bea Rebmann.

The original William B. Pierce home. Left to right: John Rebmann, Bea Rebmann and son, Tyler Rebmann, the present owners. Photo by Andrew Molloy, 1987.

The William B. Pierce home when owned by Bea and John Rebmann. Bea Rebmann in the foreground. The lay of the land slopes down from the rear of the house to the stream below. Photo by Andrew Molloy, 1987.

18

Interior of the William B. Pierce home when owned by Bea and John Rebmann. Dining Room area. Photo by Bea Rebmann, 1988.

Interior of the William B. Pierce home when owned by Bea and John Rebmann. Parlor where Augusta and Horace Tabor were married, January 31, 1857. The original ceiling still remains intact. Photo by Bea Rebmann, 1988.

Interior of the William B. Pierce home when owned by Bea and John Rebmann. Kitchen corner. Photo by Bea Rebmann, 1988.

Interior of the William B. Pierce home when owned by Bea and John Rebmann. Parlor where Augusta and Horace Tabor were married, January 31, 1857. The original metal ceiling still remains intact. Photo by Bea Rebmann, 1987.

Interior of the William B. Pierce home when owned by Bea and John Rebmann. Root cellar. Photo by Bea Rebmann, 1987.

Interior of the William B. Pierce home when owned by Bea and John Rebmann. Second floor hallway where Augusta walked over these original wide planks many times. Photo by Bea Rebmann, 1987.

21

William B. Pierce home when owned by Bea and John Rebmann. View from the rear of the house to the field below. Photo by Bea Rebmann, 1986.

William B. Pierce home when owned by Bea and John Rebmann. View from the house toward the stream. Photo by Bea Rebmann, 1986.

Pierce quarry, across the road from the old William B. Pierce home. Trees and underbrush nearly cover the site. Photo by Andrew Molloy, 1987.

Ernest M. Richardson at the Pierce quarry. Remnant of an old wagon on the site. The quarry is now full of water and leaves. Photo by Andrew Molloy, 1987.

Bea told us about something interesting in the attic. There were old newspapers pasted on the walls to keep out the cold. The dates on some of these were 1851. (Later, we will find that Augusta pasted newspapers on the walls of their Kansas homestead.) In those days, this was a popular and inexpensive method of insulating rooms.

Next day found Ernest and I at the courthouse searching through the records. It looked like a never-ending job as I surveyed the area. Many huge books, uniform in size, lined the shelves. These huge books were heavy . . . all that I could lift! Hours went by, and we worked diligently. Searching through book after book, we traced the deeds carefully. It became more exciting as progress was made. It seemed we were on the right track at last.

Ernest, with his knowledge of this type of work, zipped through the records like magic. Each time another deed was located we were spurred on to the next. The records were complete and revealed the William B. Pierce deed. It is the homestead owned by John and Bea Rebmann! Glory be! I was so happy that I jumped up and down with excitement! I was thankful to Ernest M. Richardson for his wonderful help. The Pierce quarry is across the road from the home. What a successful day! The research was extremely rewarding and now ended. At last I had everything I needed! My dream of discovery had come true.

Now everything had fallen into place!

**Futher comments about my observations of Maine in Appendix D

Almost forgotten now, the Pierce quarry is grown over with trees and bushes. The beautiful rock, once excavated here, is no longer in demand. (It is expensive building material today.) Other modern building materials can be had at much less cost. Maine has over a hundred granite quarries, but only a few are being worked on now. How sad to see the decline of the quarries. William Pierce, in his day, had a thriving business and secured the contract for erecting the State Insane Asylum in Augusta. This was, perhaps, his greatest achievement in building.

The Pierce home is well built and has an excellent rock foundation of beautiful gray granite. The high walls of the cellar are constructed of the same solid rock. I note that the blocks are perfectly cut and placed in position with great care. After all, the builder, William B. Pierce, was a stone mason, and the foundation and cellar are fine examples of his excellent work. One can see the four brick chimneys exposed in the cellar. All look in good condition. I was interested in the cellar door leading out from the back wall to the outside. Because of the sloping ground at the rear of the house, this arrangement was possible. It is convenient to use this door when bringing in vegetables to store in the root cellar.

The old Pierce homestead was built on the highest point of the property. Standing behind it, I was impressed with the good view beyond the yard to the field below. Adding to the beauty of this scene was the stream at the lower level. The trees and bushes were outstanding in their autumn colors. This was my last look at the old homestead --- a scene as pretty as a postcard. I felt sentimental about it all. Would I ever see this again?

Now, in summary, my story reveals the complete Pierce genealogy, the location of the Pierce homestead and quarry. What a busy and strenuous day this had been at the Courthouse! Back in my room at the motel, I decided to retire early. My thoughts were about the heroine of my book, Augusta Pierce.

How I did enjoy the tour of the old Pierce homestead. I was impressed with the beauty of the parlor (living room) as Bea explained the features of the room.

I thought of the dining room when the Pierces were there. A long table filled the center of the room, where there were many extra leaves, making it possible to extend the table to the length needed to accommodate the family and friends. In this household, Mrs. Pierce took in boarders from the quarry. Think of the work involved in preparing food for even one meal!

Holidays and special events took more planning and work. Each family member, as soon as they were old enough, helped with the work. Almost all food was produced on the farm. Augusta helped with the large garden, where vegetables of many varieties were grown. Lettuce and radishes were first to be ready for the table. Later, carrots, potatoes, peas, beans, cabbage, onions, turnips, beets, etc. were harvested. The children helped with meal preparation. Augusta and her brothers and sisters took turns making trips to the cellar to bring potatoes and other vegetables to the kitchen. The girls also had to peel these for cooking. Imagine the barrels of supplies in the pantry.

Sacks of flour, sugar, and corn meal; cans of lard, jams and jellies were usually on the smaller shelves. Pickles were made and kept in large stone jars. There were various ways to preserve meat; one was packing cooked meat in stone jars, covering it with hot grease. When cooled, the meat would keep until used.

One- and two- quart jars contained the home-canned fruits and vegetables. A large supply of home-canned fruits and vegetables were also on the shelves in the cellar. When butchering in winter, meat could be stored in a cold or freezing temperature and used as needed. Being able to produce almost everything they needed was like having a super market right there on the premises!

Of course, all washing of clothes was done by hand. The children all helped with dish washing. No bathrooms in those days. Wash tubs were used for bathing!

Getting children ready for school was done with much hustle and bustle. Lunches were packed and carried in dinner pails. The entire family was busy, but very happy.

There was not much time for visiting. Mrs. Pierce, and the girls, when they were older, enjoyed quilting parties. The entire family went to church. New England churches are usually white and have very high steeples . . . reaching heavenward

Fish and wild game could be had almost anytime. The Pierces raised their own farm animals. Cows furnished milk, cream, butter and cheese. Augusta helped with the chickens, where she especially liked to feed them and gather the eggs. Sometimes the hens would hide their nests, but Augusta often found them. Mrs. Pierce and her daughters were busy every day baking bread and pastries. A very pleasant aroma filled the air from the cooking and baking done in Mrs. Pierce's kitchen. Apples and blueberries were plentiful and made delicious pies.

Hungry workers from the quarry had good appetites, as did the family. The women folk were busy from morning until night. Not much was needed from the stores in the grocery line other than flour and sugar that was sold in 100 -pound sacks. Coffee was needed, and, of course, it was necessary to have kerosene for the lamps. Another daily chore for Augusta and her sisters was to keep the lamp chimneys clean and shining.

The boys helped their father with chores: cows to milk, livestock to feed and barns to clean. In addition, there was also plowing, cultivating, and finally, the harvesting in the fall.

Because of the severe winters with a lot of snow, people then stayed indoors most of the time. The barns and other buildings were attached by an ell to the house.

Some homes had a smaller kitchen attached to the regular kitchen. All buildings were connected. With this convenience, it was not necessary to go out in the cold weather.

The farm animals were kept in the barns. There was storage for hay and grain, used to feed the livestock; hay lofts were on the second floor of the barn. There was space for wagons, carriages, and other farm supplies.

Horace Austin Warner Tabor.   Photo courtesy of the State Historical Society of Colorado.

27

Birth place of Horace A. W. Tabor in Holland, Vermont. Homestead of his parents: Cornelius Dunham Tabor and Sarah (Sally) Ferrinn Tabor. This building was moved from its original location to this spot on the same farm now owned by Reginald Page. The photo and history provided by Deborah Jacobs and her family, descendants of Lemuel Tabor. Deborah's father, Kermit Jacobs, is shown standing by the building which is now used as a sugar house.

Chapter Three
Augusta Meets Horace Tabor

Years go by, and Augusta grows to be a lovely young lady. I have a copy of Augusta's own diary entitled, "Reminiscences of Mrs. Augusta Tabor." Another copy of this same diary was furnished to me by Philippe Laforgue, near Versailles, France. (He is Augusta's great grandchild.) I quote from this short autobiography as follows:

"My first acquaintance with H.A.W. Tabor came about in this way: My father, a stone contractor, wanting more stone cutters, took the train one morning for Boston. At a station 40 miles from home, two young men got on the coach that my father was on and took a seat beside him. In conversation, he remarked that he was going to Boston to hire stone cutters. They were both going to Boston to get a job! Right there and then, Father hired them, and they left the train at Portland and came home to Augusta, Maine. That was in the year of 1854." (or 1853)

Horace Austin Warner Tabor was born in Orleans County, (Holland) Vermont, on Nov. 26, 1830. He was the son of Cornelius Dunham Tabor and Sarah Ferrin Tabor. The family lived on a farm and worked diligently for a meager living. Horace was a handsome youth with a flashing eye and a ready smile; he was tall and heavily muscled from the heavy work he did on the farm.

When he was 15 or 16 years of age, his mother died. His father took another wife. Soon Horace left home to seek his fortune on his own. It is said that at age 16 he was likely working for his cousin, Martin Ferrin. Horace could see no future in farming. At age 17, he went to Quincy, Massachusetts, to learn the trade of stone-cutter. Jonathan Tabor, brother of Horace, had moved from Holland to Quincy. Horace, with the stature of a grown man, soon became a master workman.

Much to his disappointment, he received only the pay of an apprentice. Traveling around, searching for employment, he found work at various locations in New England, eventually earning the wage of a journeyman.

Horace boarded at the Pierce home and seemed satisfied with his new job at the Pierce quarry.

The William B. Pierce household was buzzing with happy voices. The evening meal was about to be served. Horace Tabor, the new man, just recently hired by Augusta's father, seemed to fit right in with the family and other employees. "They are all in a jolly mood," remarked Augusta's sister , Lucy.

"Father says Horace is a good worker . . . so big and strong" commented sister Rebecca.

"Come girls, let's get the food to the table," ordered Mrs. Pierce. Family and quarry workers were all in their places at the long dining room table. Mother Pierce and daughters were busy in the kitchen. "Where is Augusta?" asked Mrs. Pierce.

"Oh, she has gone back upstairs for the second time to fix her hair," answered sister Ruth. Just then Augusta appeared in the kitchen.

"I can't get my curls arranged right," complained Augusta.

"Strange that she should be concerned about her hair now when we are so busy," mumbled Mother Pierce. Augusta was beaming as she smoothed her apron, ready to help wait on tables. She wanted to look her best and was anxious to impress Horace.

There was a hot fire in the black kitchen range. As usual, Mrs. Pierce and her daughters had been busy for hours cooking and preparing food for supper. Augusta's eyes were on the new face at the table, that of Horace Tabor.

Isn't he handsome! thought Augusta, as she placed a large plate of biscuits on the table. Horace seemed to enjoy all the family, but he especially kept looking at Augusta. Rebecca noticed that Augusta seemed a bit nervous as she poured hot steaming coffee into the large heavy coffee cups.

"That coffee smells so good," remarked Horace, watching Augusta fill his cup. Lucy and Augusta carried more platters of food to the table. Soon the table was loaded. Everyone had good appetites.

When supper was over and the dishes were done, all retired to the parlor. Horace and Augusta were seated off in a corner, having a wonderful visit. Horace was telling all about Vermont. "I am so glad to have steady work at your father's quarry," said Horace. "It is wonderful to have a boarding place so close to the quarry too," he added.

"What a coincidence that you and my father should be on the same train at the same time!" remarked Augusta.

Life continued on in this peaceful setting for the next two years. It was evident that Augusta and Horace were very much in love. In fact, it was love at first sight!

Horace spent evenings after work and Sundays with Augusta. They enjoyed the usual young people's church activities such as ice cream socials and an occasional hay ride party.

In summer, a favorite spot for the young lovers was the beautiful back yard. Here they would sit for hours under a huge tree, enjoying each other's company.

As mentioned previously, a short distance from the house the level area of the ground took an abrupt slant, almost vertical. It eventually sloped to the garden area and field below. At the lowest point of the property, and beyond, was the winding river. Now, nature was at its best with trees and shrubs blending into the distance.

In this setting, Augusta and Horace often walked down the worn pathway to the beautiful river below. There Horace carved their initials in the bark of a large tree encircled with the shape of a heart. They had long conversations . . . dreaming about the future. One beautiful evening Horace proposed to Augusta. She was thrilled, and they were both very happy. They knew that the sensible decision to be made was to wait until Horace could save more money and then get married.

Horace had always enjoyed reading about the West and especially gold discoveries in California. "I've been reading that article you gave me about the gold discoveries in California," said Augusta. "I can understand how you enjoy dreaming of being there yourself," she added.

Augusta had caught some of Horace's excitement, but one evening she said, "It is such a long way to California. You have a good job here in the quarry. Let us save money for a home of our own right here near our family and friends," reasoned Augusta in her most serious manner.

This settled Horace for a time, but one Sunday afternoon he was filled with even more enthusiasm about the future. "The New England Emigrant Aid Company is still helping people go west," stated Horace. "My brother John thinks Kansas Territory is a good place to take a homestead," he added.

"Yes, John has taken a claim near Lawrence," said Augusta. "Let us wait and see how he does before you get any ideas about going there," advised Augusta.

"Oh, my dear Augusta, please listen to me. I want to go West to seek a fortune," pleaded Horace. "As soon as I have a homestead and am well established in that new territory, I shall come back for you, and we will marry and start life together in the West!"

Horace was determined to go, and Augusta had to now see it his way. They were engaged, but marriage had to wait until Horace tried his hand as a farmer on the American frontier. (Jonathan is thought to have been instrumental in influencing Horace to leave his trade of stonecutter and head for Kansas.)

Chapter Four
Pioneer Life In Deep Creek

Horace A.W. Tabor left Vermont with the 1855 spring party of the New England Emigrant Aid Company that left Boston on March 13. This group was under the leadership of Dr. Charles Robinson. The Emigrant companies were organized to encourage people to go West, thus the country would be settled with anti-slavery people. This would prevent the spread of slavery into this new territory.

In 1855, there was a struggle in Kansas between the free-state and slave-state people. Most of the free-state emigrants settled near Lawrence. Horace's brother, John, had already taken a claim near Lawrence. Horace decided to follow his brother John and go to the Kansas Territory. It seemed a good opportunity, as the Emigrant Aid Company would help the settlers financially. It was also an adventure and a chance to make a better living.

Josiah H. Pillsbury had preceded Horace Tabor to Kansas. He was not satisfied with what he saw near Lawrence. He traveled on west many miles away from any settlement. Here he found what he wanted on Deep Creek in Riley County.

It was a choice location and had natural beauty, including a waterfall. Flat rock, in one place, was ideal for a safe crossing, when fording the river. This site was named Pillsbury Crossing.

Valleys of the Kansas River and Deep Creek were well known for producing excellent crops. Mr. Pillsbury named the settlement Zeandale. The word is a combination of the Greek work "Zea" meaning corn, and "dale" an English word. Thus, the name corn dale or corn valley fits the description of the area.

Pillsbury Crossing settlers were going to build a town there to be named Pillsbury, but the plans never did materialize.

Josiah Pillsbury had journeyed back to Kansas City to meet relatives waiting for him there. His plans were to take them to his claim on Deep Creek. At this point, Horace Tabor and four other men met the Pillsbury group.

Soon, arrangements were made to join Mr. Pillsbury. It was 100 miles to Deep Creek. They had several yokes of oxen, but only one wagon. The wagon was loaded with their supplies: axes, shovels, plows, bedding, food, tents, and ammunition for their "Beecher Bibles."

Travel was difficult, and they only averaged ten miles a day. They were glad to be on their way to the Pillsbury claim. Upon their arrival, the men agreed they had never seen a more desirable land. "This is where we will settle and build our cabins," said Horace.

Horace Tabor and the other men worked, building a cabin for Josiah Pillsbury first of all. Mr. Pillsbury was physically unable to do heavy work, but he helped the others with lighter and necessary work.

When the cabin was completed, the other men selected their own 160 acre sites. Horace took his land about five miles south of Zeandale. He lived in a dugout against a bank above the creek until his own cabin could be built. Later, he moved up on a slope, on a hill, to build a cabin. This area is called Mount Tabor.

The men joined together and built a cabin on each man's claim. They cut black walnut logs from the wealth of timber at Deep Creek. The cabin was 12' x 16'. (The smallest the law allowed was 10' x 12'.) By fall all the best land along the stream had been taken by other emigrants arriving in the area.

The winter of 1855 was cold, bringing 20 to 30 degree below zero. The settlers were not prepared for this weather, as the previous winter had been mild. Their cabins were not built good enough to keep out the cold, as they had been informed that the winters were fairly mild. They suffered through it all.

Years later, recollections of hardy pioneers were made when Horace Tabor was a settler on Deep Creek. An incident from "Log Cabin Days", Riley County Historical Society is recorded as follows,

". . .one winter morning in 1856 when he (Horace) made an early morning call at our cabin. He was walking home from some neighbors place, and was carrying a coffee mill under his arm. One of us said we had been wondering if he had starved out during the hard freezing weather just past.

His laugh roared out as he answered: "You needn't worry about Horace Tabor starving while he has plenty of corn and a coffee mill to grind it in."

News spread in December that pro-slavery men were preparing to attack Lawrence. Horace Tabor, with his rifle, set out on foot to join the anti-slavery men. It was a long, weary march over a hundred miles. In three days he was there and helped defend the town.

Upon his return to Deep Creek, his neighbors praised him and what he had done. They saw that he had courage, intelligence and initiative.

By now he had the reputation of being a genial and friendly young man. He had shown his willingness to help his neighbors. Horace was elected as a representative of his district to the first Kansas Free State legislature in Topeka; also, he was a member of the County Board of Commissioners.

Horace came west to farm, but to his surprise found himself in politics.

In the meantime, our heroine, back in Augusta, Maine, was very lonesome. During the separation from her handsome Horace, she kept busy helping with the family duties. She longed to see the man of her dreams, but tried to be cheerful.

She always looked for a letter from Horace. His letters were short, but at least she kept posted as to his progress in building the cabin, getting involved in politics and life in general on the frontier. There was never a word about his being homesick, but he was pining to see Augusta. He kept assuring her that he would soon return.

Horace returned to Augusta, Maine, and was reunited with his bride-to-be. Their marriage was to be on January 31, 1857, and would take place in the Pierce parlor where they first met. Horace was 26 years of age, and Augusta was 23 years old.

Chapter Five
The Wedding

"Morning at last," whispered Augusta to herself. She was awake before dawn, and not a soul was stirring this dark winter night. She tiptoed quietly down the front stairway. Stepping into the parlor, she lit the lamp, paused a moment in front of the fireplace, and musing to herself, said, "Just think, we will be married right here, today! The very place where Horace and I met in 1854. Along life's way, another door is opening, and where will it lead?" she asked in silence.

Yes, the most eventful day in the lives of young Augusta and Horace had arrived, Jan. 31, 1857, their wedding day. It was almost daylight, and now everyone was up and busy with their own household duties. Father Pierce and the boys were busy with the heaters and range. Some fires had nearly burned out, and it was necessary to rebuild them. Glowing coals remained under the ashes, and the fire was easily revived. In some rooms, with smaller heaters, the fire had completely gone out, and the boys had to fetch kindling and wood to build the fires over again. Soon the house was comfortably warmed, and the fire in the kitchen range burned brightly.

Next, Mr. Pierce and the boys milked the cows and finished the outside chores. Mother Pierce and the daughters were busy preparing breakfast. There was no lingering at the breakfast table this morning, as there were many things to accomplish before the wedding.

For weeks the girls had been cleaning house and decorating the rooms. The parlor looked especially attractive. House plants were doing well and added to the beauty of the home. A huge Christmas cactus was still in bloom and outdoing all of the other plants.

The Pierce flower gardens were beautiful during the summer. By autumn, Augusta and her sisters had dried many of these lovely blossoms for winter use. 'Everlasting' variety was a favorite. Vases were filled with these colorful flowers. Augusta had created the loveliest of all the bouquets. Mother Pierce placed it on the center table in the parlor and said to Augusta, "It is truly a work of art!"

Every piece of furniture in the house had been polished to perfection. The organ had its prominent place in the parlor and seemed to be just waiting for the organist to play "The Wedding March."

The pleasant odor of a variety of foods filled the air. Cooking and baking had been going on for several weeks. The Pierces were now prepared for the reception that would follow the wedding.

Mr. Pierce peeked into the kitchen just in time to see his wife and daughters adding the finishing touches to the three-tiered wedding cake. "That white frosting turned out perfectly," said Mother Pierce, as she added the last bit of frosting to the cake. The boys were waiting in the background, ready to lick the spoon and pan.

Lucy had placed the best linen table cloth on the dining room table. Mother Pierce put the cake in the center of the table and stepped back as they all gazed at the work of art, complete with tiny candy trim. "Oh Mother," exclaimed Augusta, "I didn't know the cake would be that huge."

"We are expecting all the relatives and many friends, so we need a lot of food," replied her mother. Homemade ice cream was a treat in those days. A large freezer full was ready to add to the dessert course. Ice cream was easily kept frozen in the January weather.

Mother Pierce, a very talented seamstress, had spent many hours making Augusta's wedding gown. The dress and bridal veil were fashioned of white fine silk with tiny ribbon trim. The veil was also styled with a lace-like net. The skirt of the dress hung in graceful fullness from the small waistline to the floor -length hem. The blending beauty of the train gave the gown the desired effect of elegance.

All the Pierce family, now dressed in their Sunday best attire, anxiously awaited the wedding. Augusta was still in her bedroom; Mother and sisters by her side, helping her get dressed.

Mother Pierce held out a string of pearls and said, "Here, my dear, wear my pearls for this wonderful occasion,"

"Oh, thank you Mother," exclaimed Augusta, putting her arms around her mother and giving her a hug and kiss. At last the bride was ready.

Mother Pierce stood back with folded hands held under her chin. She gazed at her daughter in silence and then said, "Seems only yesterday that you were only a wisp of a girl, and now you are a beautiful bride." Mother wiped a tear from her eye and disappeared to the kitchen to check on the food preparation.

Augusta's sisters were bouncing around the room in great excitement, chattering about the wedding and trying to help the bride. Augusta seemed calm and didn't have time to get nervous.

Mrs. Pierce had taken time to make a beautiful suit for Horace. It was tailored perfectly, and he was very handsome in this fashionable outfit. He was most grateful to Mrs. Pierce and said to her, "I've never had a real suit like this!"

Horace was ready for the wedding. Mr. Pierce helped him adjust his new tie. Glancing in a mirror for a final check, he seemed a bit nervous, but proudly hurried to the parlor.

The wedding guests were already arriving. The house was crowded. Expressions of happiness were on all faces, and laughter filled the air.

Father Pierce looked very proper in his best suit. He stood at the front entrance awaiting his daughter's appearance at the head of the stairway. "There she is!" he exclaimed. He smiled, and with the expression of a proud Father, he said, "You are lovely, my dear, and the gown is beautiful!"

The bride carefully descended the stairs and took her father's arm. Mother Pierce was in her very best dress for this event. She also looked beautiful. "The Wedding March!" exclaimed Augusta, as the organ music filled the air.

"Come, my dear daughter " said Father Pierce as they started for the parlor. Augusta walked slowly, every movement was graceful. Horace stood filled with awe, as he saw his bride enter the room. How beautiful! She was adorned in such splendor!

Augusta was of slender build, straight posture and overflowing with vitality. What a delightful young lady she was with curly hair and a soft voice. She took her place by his side, and he whispered in her ear, "My darling sweetheart." There they were, the bride and the bridegroom. What a perfect couple! Horace beamed with happiness with Augusta beside him. She was the love of his life!

The minister spoke in a clear voice as the wedding ceremony began. The guests looked on as the marriage vows were spoken. When the ceremony was over, Horace kissed the bride. Relatives and friends crowded near the handsome couple to wish them a happy marriage.

There were many wonderful gifts yet to unwrap, such as silverware, dishes, and kitchen utensils. Many gifts were handmade. It was a stormy winter day, but indoors all were filled with happiness, and a merry time was had by all.

Horace and Augusta were well suited to each other, and together, were capable of accepting the challenge of pioneer life. Horace was a tall, lean and powerful man with broad shoulders and muscular arms. He was a handsome youth and kind and generous. He was always ready to help a friend.

The early years of Augusta, in that rugged country, did much to produce and develop the strong character she possessed and maintained her entire life. Not only did the environment have its effects on Augusta, but her good upbringing by her parents was a great advantage.

They had little money, but with the advantage of youth, good health and courage, they were sure to succeed.

Her good qualities of character were strong enough to later lead her successfully through life, later culminating in the Colorado Rockies!

Augusta packed only one trunk and took along small items she could carry with Horace's baggage. They were ready to start for the West. They took only necessary items as freight charges were expensive in those days. Leaving the Pierce home on February 25, Augusta left the comforts of her happy New England home to share with Horace the trials and hardships of life on the rugged American frontier.

Prairie schooner headed west over the rolling prairies. The white cover of the prairie schooner, swaying over the sea of grass, looks like a boat on the water, which probably accounts for the name.

Tabor Homestead. A log cabin, constructed of black walnut logs, was the first home built by H. A. W. Tabor near Zeandale, Kansas. It no longer exists. Shown here is the second home of the Tabor's, built of white limestone. Note the wooden additions by later owners. This home is still standing. Photo by Evelyn Furman, 1969.

Chapter Six
Heading West

Even though railroad travel was slow, tiresome and hazardous, it was still better than going by wagon. The Tabors were happy to be on their way. Sharp curves and weak bridges added to the risk involved in such a journey. Occasionally, livestock wandered onto the tracks, often forcing the trains to a dead stop. Finally, the tracks were cleared and the train struggled on at the usual speeds of ten, fifteen or perhaps twenty miles per hour. Coaches were dusty and sooty. Hard seats were anything but comfortable, but travelers, then, knew nothing better.

They were glad to see modes of transportation improving. In larger cities it was necessary to transfer from one railroad to another. The stations or depots were sometimes a mile or more apart. Sleeping or dining cars were still a thing of the future. Most people carried lunches or fruit packed in a shoe box, or some sort of container. Food purchased at railroad lunch counters was expensive.

The first leg of the trip took them to the end of the tracks in St. Louis. After the tiresome seven-day train ride, another two days would be spent on a Missouri River steamboat headed for Kansas City. Horace had saved enough money to purchase needed items in Kansas City, which were: a yoke of oxen, a wagon, farming tools, seeds, and some staples. It was then on to Deep Creek, which was 100 miles westward.

I quote from Augusta's diary: "We were nearly three weeks going from Kansas City to Zeandale. The cattle were thin and the grass poor. There came with us from Augusta, Maine, two gentlemen ."

They were Samuel B. Kellogg and Nathaniel Maxcy, also emigrants from New England and friends of the Tabors. They joined in on the trip to Deep Creek. All men were armed and carried their weapons openly. This insured their safety in Kansas City and was adequate protection all the way to Deep Creek. They were welcome travelers." The old saying, "there is safety in numbers" held true here.

I quote from the <u>Manhattan Kansas Mercury</u>", March 9, 1935: "The roads west of Kansas City were not entirely safe for a free state man traveling alone. Tabor was glad to have the company of his friends. Both were brave men and accurate shots with their Sharps rifles.

For the first few days, while passing through pro-slavery settlements, Mrs. Tabor guided the oxen while the men marched beside the wagon on foot, their rifles ready for instant use. They arrived at Deep Creek on April 19.

It rained nearly every day, which made the roads almost impassable. The young bride was tired, homesick, frightened, and disgusted. The final straw was when she saw the sort of home Tabor had provided. It was located on the flat, open prairie, with not a house, a stone, or a tree anywhere in sight."

Manhattan was about eight miles distant. Augusta thought this was a desolate place, and she disliked the Kansas wind blowing furiously. The Tabor cabin was about a half a mile from any other cabin and was 12 x 16 feet in size.

Augusta's diary revealed that she was ushered into the cabin, and the first thing she saw was a No. 7 cook stove. She sat down upon an old trunk, the only thing to sit on, and the tears began to flow, "Why I felt so badly I could not tell, for I had not been deceived. I knew just the size of the house; I also knew that it stood out upon an open prairie. I could not realize how lonely it could be."

This was the breaking point for Augusta! Under great stress, she broke down and cried. After a few hours she dried her tears. Now that she had regained her composure, she once again faced the reality of the circumstances confronting her.

She never once thought of defeat, not Augusta! She was determined to remain by the side of the man she loved. Horace was fortunate in having a mate with such stamina. Augusta, an educated, cultured woman, felt helpless in this open country. However, she was out of her element.

The Pierces were a determined and respected family; therefore, Augusta vowed she would help Horace make this venture a success. After all, President Franklin Pierce was her cousin. Augusta was modest, and not one to boast of the Pierce achievements; she also had courage, which carried her through her entire life, as we shall see . . .

In a few months the Tabor baby would arrive; however, a surgeon could be had only at Fort Riley, which was twenty miles away. There was no woman in the immediate vicinity to help Augusta, consequently, she was panic stricken, but she would make the best of it some way.

In retrospect, let us review the circumstances in Augusta's young life as a bride. In the past, some biographers refer to her as frail and sickly. What she had just experienced is enough to make any strong woman ill.

In fairness to Augusta, I offer these facts to be considered: Augusta, like Horace, was in good health when she left Maine. The trip to Deep Creek was a great hardship. Some emigrants were known to have given up and turned back to their homes in New England. Others perished along the way; some settlers that finally were established, later died of ague.

There were those that were killed in Indian raids or met death from the gun fire of the pro-slavery element, not to mention those that were killed by wild animals.

As for the Tabors, often unfavorable weather conditions added to the struggle. Roads were only trails over these prairies. There were no bridges over the streams, and many of the fords were deep and treacherous. Nevertheless, they forged ahead!

Augusta, being pregnant, was under added strain. In her condition it was unfortunate that she was subjected to such difficult circumstances. Augusta, because of necessity, continued to guide the oxen on part of the trip.

She was a brave young lady, not knowing when they would face gunfire from any direction. The pro-slavery element was "on the watch." At times they (the settlers) were followed by Indians. The Indians and snakes were a constant worry to Augusta.

The immediate concern was to get settled in the cabin and start the farming venture.

Augusta rallied to the side of Horace, always a faithful helpmate and the love of his life.

Horace and the other two men unloaded the wagon. He made three-legged stools, a table, and put up a shelf for dishes.

Augusta busied herself cleaning up the cabin, and "prepared the first meal that I ever tried to cook." She removed her table linen and silver from her trunk. She left home with the usual outfit given a bride. Most of the wedding gifts were left in Maine, because not much baggage could be taken on the trip west.

Augusta knew the fundamentals of cooking, but was not accustomed to the conditions she now faced. At home, in Maine, Augusta helped in the kitchen. Now she did the cooking with the help of the two friends, Samuel B. Kellogg and Nathaniel Maxcy. With their help, Augusta managed to prepare what food they had. It was a meager meal, but they were all very hungry. In Maine, the Pierce home was well stocked with a variety of foods. Now it was necessary to adjust to a very simple diet and method of cooking.

The two friends were kind to Augusta, and she welcomed their assistance. They were boarders, and the money they paid would be a supplement to the Tabor income. The menu was usually hog and hominy, with corn bread and milk for a change.

Years later, in retrospect, Augusta said, "I cannot say it was a very inviting meal, but I did the best I could, and we were all blessed with good appetites."

There was a rough bedstead made of poles, on which was an old tick filled with prairie grass. Augusta found New York Tribune newspapers in the cabin and put them to good use. With a flour and water paste, she applied them to the log walls, placing them right side up so she could read them at her leisure. (Reading material was scarce.) Next, she unpacked the boxes and made up a decent bed.

Horace fell trees, hauled logs, and made a shelter for the oxen. With the two young and strong oxen, Horace broke the land and began planting seed. He had a large field of corn. He was now farming in earnest. He exchanged a days labor with neighbors to save hiring help.

Augusta wanted a garden, so Horace built a rail fence around the garden plot. He also constructed a fox-proof coop and runway for the chickens. Augusta looked after the garden and chickens and prepared meals for Horace and the two boarders. After Augusta finished her housework, she too worked in the fields. Alas, there was no rain that summer, and thus no crops.

Horace went to Fort Riley and worked at his trade.

A baby boy was born on October 9, 1857. He was named Nathaniel Maxcy. Now Augusta was busy with the care of her baby and made a little money raising chickens.

Rattle snakes crawled into the cabin to get into the shade, so Augusta learned to only sit on a three-legged stool with her feet under her because of her fear of the snakes. The snakes also crawled upon her bed and her milk shelves. Kansas was alive with snakes!

In the spring of 1859, farming was tried again. This was a good year and there was an abundant crop, but no market. Eggs were three cents per dozen and shelled corn was twenty cents per bushel. Augusta kept boarders and made butter to sell.

In February 1859, Horace learned of the Pike's Peak Gold Rush. Some of Green Russell's party was returning from Colorado and spread the news. Horace decided at once to try his luck in the New Eldorado.

Horace told Augusta that she might go home to Maine, but she refused to leave him. She felt her place was with her husband. Horace, on second thought, decided it would be more profitable to take Augusta, as then they would continue to have the two boarders. Money from them would keep them all in basic provisions. Mr. Tabor worked at the Fort through March and April to earn money for the outfit to go west.

May 5, they left Zeandale. They yoked the oxen and cows, and included was a pair of year-old steers. They purchased supplies sufficient for a few months. Their belongings were packed and the wagon loaded, and all was made ready for the journey. Augusta and the baby rode in the wagon; the three men rode in the front, on the seat provided there, with Horace as the driver.

Plans were to return in the fall or when they had made enough money to pay for the 160 acres of land and buy a little herd of cattle.

Tabor School, Zeandale, Kansas, is still in existence.   Photo by Lucille Duffin, 1987.

IN MEMORY OF AUGUSTA PIERCE
TABOR A PIONEER MOTHER WHO
WITH HER HUSBAND H.A.W.TABOR
SETTLED HERE IN 1856 AND GAVE
THIS BEAUTIFUL VALLEY THE NAME
"TABOR VALLEY"

IN 1859 THEY MOVED ON TO THE
ROCKY MOUNTAINS AND FOUND
THE RICHES OF GOLCONDA AND
THEIR HISTORY WILL BE A LEGEND
IN COLORADO FOREVER

THIS MONUMENT ERECTED TO THEIR
MEMORY BY THE CENTENNIAL
COMMITTEE OF MANHATTAN KANS.
APRIL 1955

Tabor Monument, in memory of Augusta Pierce Tabor, is located in front of the Tabor schoolhouse, near the Tabor homestead, Zeandale, Kansas -- now known as Tabor Valley.

45

Chapter Seven
A Trip To Tabor Valley

On November 28,1969, my husband, Gordon Furman, and I made a trip to Kansas. I had decided to do research in Zeandale where the Tabors had homesteaded. Arriving first in Manhattan, we located the courthouse to get copies of any Tabor deeds available. We also visited the local museum, which was interesting. We had directions to Zeandale, but were told there was nothing left there but one boarded-up store building. We found that, but drove around the area a long time before locating the Tabor homestead.

I inquired along the way at each farmhouse, but no one had heard of the place or the name Tabor. I was determined to find the spot, so kept looking. As we were very near to the end of our search, people living in neighboring farmhouses were able to give us directions. Finally, the stone house was located about four miles from Zeandale.

I have a copy of an old letter written by Emily Tabor, a sister of Horace Tabor. She relates how she had visited the old homestead years later after Horace and Augusta had moved away. At this time she discovered that the old original, walnut log cabin was gone. This letter, in part; from E. J. Moyes (sister of Horace Tabor) Lawrence, Kansas, 331 Indiana St., October 20, 1891, written to Elizabeth (Baby Doe), the second wife of Horace Tabor:

> Dear Sister Lizzie,
> "I walked all over the farm . . . Saw a few rocks where the old cabin was where Horace lived so long ago. Also saw a stone house Horace built . . . at that time. Saw the mountain called Tabor Mountain, and the creek is Tabor Creek and a lovely valley nearby is Tabor Valley. Sunday evening we went to a school house to church. It is Tabor Valley school house. I have a few pretty rocks. Triphena (was the wife of Lamuel Tabor . . . brother of Horace.) had picked up on Tabors mountain . . . all these places named for Horace so long ago. All the old neighbors there speak in such an admirable way of Horace.

46

. . . It is a real nice country school house with organ and globe and other things for a good school.

The property is now owned by John Howard Akin. It is occupied by his parents, Mr. & Mrs. Del Mar Akin. Mrs. Akin responded to my knock on the door. We introduced ourselves and told her of our mission. She seemed interested and very friendly.

"Do come in," she said, opening wide the door. A very interesting conversation ensued, and I was delighted to learn that she knew the history of the area and also about the Tabors.

She told us how to find the dugout where Horace stayed when he first came to Deep Creek. "Oh yes, it's on the Kimball farm" she said. "You will also pass by Tabor Creek, which runs through the farm. This second house is built of white limestone," she said.

I could see that an addition had been built on each side of the four exterior walls. One addition was a kitchen and the rest were bedrooms. An inside stairway led up to another room used as an attic now, but was once a bedroom.

Next, she took us out through the kitchen door and showed us the Tabor well. (It is not in use now,) and it was covered with a large heavy stone slab. She said it was originally a bucket-type well. We walked around to the back of the house, and Mrs. Akin pointed to a huge hill area. "That is Mount Tabor," she informed us. I was busy with my camera trying to get pictures of everything of interest.

Mrs. Akin went on to tell me what she had heard of the Tabor story. She described Horace as being "tall, lean, and powerfully built." He was genial and generous with what he had, whether it was much or little. He was always ready to help a friend in need. His faults were procrastination and extravagance.

Then she mentioned Augusta as being "a woman of education, culture, and courage."

Those living in that area tell how Horace made friends easily. They are proud to tell how he was elected as representative from his district to the Topeka legislature in 1856. He was a member of the House of Representatives and elected to the County Board of Commissioners. (She continued with other history we have read and is recorded in Colorado.)

She told me about the hardships of the settlers. In wet season there was much fever and ague --- Kansas brand of ague. The sick person was taken with a chill. Quinine was used in extreme cases. Some settlers got so homesick that it really did make them ill. The excitement and stress caused by the many dangers of the early day could be enough to make anyone ill. There were few doctors, and neighbors had to help each other in times of sickness.

The stone school house, built in 1882, was named for the Tabors. It is a half mile west of the stone house. (It was boarded up when we were there.) Only a piano and globe of the world remained inside. It was made a Community Center after the school was closed. The district joined the Zeandale district in 1960.

We were happy to see this building still standing there in Tabor Valley. It was named in honor of Augusta and Horace A. W. Tabor, who built their cabin on the creek which is a tributary to Deep Creek. A marble marker was erected in front of the school house by the Historical Centennial Committee of Manhattan, Kansas, in 1955.

Engraved on the stone is an inscription as follows: "In memory of Augusta Pierce Tabor, a pioneer mother, who, with her husband H.A.W. Tabor, settled here in 1856 and gave this beautiful valley the name of Tabor Valley." Augusta is in the limelight here! It is most appropriate that this beautiful monument should be erected in honor of Augusta. I was favorably impressed as I stood there in silence, thinking back to the early times of the Tabors.

Early Colorado-pioneer history records Horace Tabor as being the most famous and colorful character of the time. The millions he made impressed the world with his rapid success in mining.

Another look at the Tabors, and we see Augusta, not just as the underlying support of Horace in all his endeavors, but now at the forefront herself. Without Augusta, the Tabor story might have been very different. Augusta was the real mainstay of Horace. She, in her own right, must be given recognition for the wonderful person that she was. In the eyes of those in this new West, she rightly deserved the attention she received.

I quote Augusta from Tales of the Colorado Pioneers by Alice Polk Hill: "I feel that in those years of self-sacrifice, hard labor, and economy, I laid the foundation to Mr. Tabor's immense wealth; for, had I not stayed with him and worked by his side, he would have been discouraged, returned to his trade, and so lost the opportunity which has since enriched him."

As we walked around the old school house, I turned to Mrs. Akin and remarked, "I hope this Tabor School will survive and not be destroyed. It looks to be a very solid-built structure, even today. By the way, who owns the building?" I inquired.

"Mr. Glenn Vilander," answered Mrs. Akin. Then she related this story to me as follows: "His name was really Johnson. There were eight brothers that came to this country and registered their names."

The official in charge had many Johnsons in his book, and he said, "Can't some of you give me some other name?"

"I *come here buy land*," explained one of the Johnson's. 'Buyland' sounded like 'Viland,' so the officer recorded his name as such. He got that name for keeps. "The rest of the brothers are all Johnson," said Mrs. Akin.

How interesting, I thought.

"Would you like to see Pillsbury Crossing?" asked Mrs. Akin as I was preparing to leave.

"Oh, yes!" I exclaimed.

"Let me tell you a story about Horace Tabor," said Mrs. Akin.

"Please do," I answered.

"Well, this happened on the day the Tabors left for the West. Their wagon was loaded and all ready to depart. Horace's last words were, as he pulled off his boots, "I'm emptying the Kansas dust out of my shoes."

The wagon rumbled over Pillsbury Crossing for the last time. "Colorado, here I come," shouted Horace as he swung his hat high over his head. With farewells to their friends, they joined the Pike's Peak Gold Rush. The wagon disappeared slowly and faded into the distance.

I thanked Mrs. Akin for the tour of her house, the outside points of interest, her information and stories. We said our good-byes, and returned to our motel in the Holiday Inn in Manhattan. It was Thanksgiving, and we had a very fine dinner there. As we sat there enjoying our meal, I kept wondering what the Tabors had to eat for their Thanksgiving dinners here in Tabor Valley long ago. I had many things to be thankful for, and our experience in Tabor Valley in 1969 was certainly one of them.

49

Chapter Eight
From Kansas And Denver To California Gulch

I quote from <u>Tales of the Colorado Pioneers</u>, by Alice Polk Hill and Augusta's own diary:

"What I endured on this journey only the women who crossed the plains in '59 can realize. There was no station until we arrived within eighty miles of Denver via the Republican route. There was no road a good part of the way and no fuel. I was weak and feeble, having nearly shaken myself to death with fever and ague in Kansas. The Indians were all along the route, but friendly. But all Indians, like snakes, are the same to me. I lived in constant dread of them. I had to cook for all our party, and I did not find it a pleasure. Sometimes the wind would blow furiously, and it is not very pleasant to cook over a campfire in a wind storm when that fire is made of buffalo chips and every gust of wind would carry them over the barren prairie. By the time I would get them gathered together, another puff, and so on, lasting three or four days. We were obliged to gather buffalo chips, sometimes traveling miles to find enough chips to cook a meal. This weary work fell to the women, for the men had enough to do in taking care of the teams, and in making and breaking the camp. The Indians followed us all the time, and though friendly, were continually begging and stealing.

Every Sunday we rested, if rest it could be called. The men went hunting, while I stayed to guard the camp, wash the soiled linen and cook for the following week. Quite frequently the Indians gathered around my camp, so that I could do nothing all day. They wallowed in the water sources from which our supplies were obtained, and were generally very filthy. My babe was teething and suffering from fever and ague, so that he required constant attention day and night. My weight was only ninety pounds."

I continue with information on Mrs. Augusta Tabor from <u>Tales of the Colorado Pioners</u>" by Alice Polk Hill and "Reminiscences of Mrs. Augusta Tabor", her own diary, the same copy given me by Philippe Laforgue of France.

We arrived in Denver about the middle of June. We camped on the Platte River near where the West Side Bridge now stands. The cattle were footsore. We were obliged to camp there until the first day of July. Then we went up Clear Creek where the town of Golden was being established. A miner came down from the mountains from whom we inquired the way to Gregory diggings. Leaving me and my sick child in the 7x9 tent, that my hands had made, the men took a supply of provisions on their backs, a few blankets, and bidding me be good to myself, left on the morning of the glorious Fourth. How sadly I felt, none but God, in whom I then firmly trusted, knew. Twelve miles from a human soul save my babe. The only sound I heard was the lowing of the cattle, and they, poor things, seemed to feel the loneliness of our situation, and kept unusually quiet. Every morning and evening I had a round-up all to myself. There were no cowboys for me to cut, slash and shoot, no disputing of brands or mavericks. Three long, weary weeks I held the fort. At the expiration of that time, they returned. On the twenty-sixth of July we again loaded the wagon and started into the mountains. The road was a mere trail; every few rods we were obliged to stop and widen it so as to get the wagon through on many hills we were obliged to take every thing from the wagon and then help the oxen to get the wagon up, the men carrying the goods as best they could. Going down hill was so much easier that it was often necessary to fasten a full grown pine tree to the back of the wagon for a hold-back or brake. Often night overtook us where it was impossible to find a level place to spread a blanket. Under such circumstances, we drove stakes in the ground, rolled a log against them, and lay with our feet against the log and sleep, oh, so sweetly, with Mother Earth for a bed and the blue sky for a roof. Sometimes the fill was so steep that we slept almost upright. We were nearly three weeks cutting our way through Russell's Gulch into Payne's Bar, now called Idaho Springs.

"Ours was the first wagon through, and I was the first white woman there, if white I could be called after camping out three months. We arrived there about the middle or 20th of August. There were no women there, but many prospectors. The men cut trees or logs, laid them up four feet in height, then put the 7x9 tent on for a roof making me a comfortable house. Mr. Tabor went on to a Spanish Bar and went to prospecting. I opened an eating house and

51

bakery, made pies and bread to sell. Sold milk from the cows we had driven across the plains . . . gave meals.

Here one of our party, Mr. Maxcy, had an attack of mountain fever, and for four weeks he lay, very ill, at the door of our tent, in a wagon bed, I acting as physician and nurse. A miner with a gunshot wound through his hand was also brought to my door for attention. I was busy every moment from early morn until late at night, finding much more than busy hands could do.

With the 25th of September came the first snow, a few inches. An old miner came to our camp who told us dreadful stories of snow slides, and advised Mr. Tabor to take me out of the mountains immediately. Those who know anything of the surroundings of Idaho Springs will smile at the idea of a snow slide there. But we, in our ignorance of mountains believed all the old miner said. We had never seen a mountain, only as we passed through the Alleghenies en route West. We pulled our tent and left for Denver.

I had been very successful with my bakery and eating house. I had what we called a profitable summer. Made enough to pay for the farm in Kansas, and to keep us through the winter.

Had found a trustworthy young man that would take the money and a dog that we had brought with us from home, one that I had raised back on the farm in Kansas. I did not feel able to feed the dog through the winter with the cheapest article of food that could be bought at 25 cents a pound and upward. So with many a sigh, I parted with my faithful dog "Patty."

Arriving in Denver, we rented a room over Vasques' store. There was one window, a rough board floor, the roof reached to the floor. We paid $25 a month. It was the first roof I had slept under for six months. I took a few boarders. Mr. Tabor returned to his prospect, which he found had been jumped by the miner who had advised us to leave. "Might was right" in those days, so he lost all his summers work, and had to sell the cow to buy the supply for the new camp which was up the headwaters of the Arkansas.

The 19th of February, 1860, I was lifted from a bed of sickness to a wagon; we left Denver and started for the new mining excitement. No woman had yet been there. This time taking four men along we were four to seven days going to where Manitou now stands. I made biscuits with the water of the soda springs, they were yellow and tasted so strongly of soda that even we with our outdoor appetites, could not relish them. We lingered there one week, the men doing a little prospecting and working on a new road over Ute Pass. We started up into the mountains over the new road and for several days we made such slow progress that we could look back to the last

52

night's camp smoke. The men worked hard to get the first wagon over the road. The weather was changeable . . . a few inches of snow falling nearly every night. I speak of this, for it made it wet and sloppy cooking over a campfire, and my health was very poor that spring. We were two long, weary weeks getting up to the South Park. I shall never forget how beautiful the park looked when I first beheld it. The sun was just setting, its beautiful rays reflected back, tinging the whole heavens with crimson and yellow clouds. It looked like a cultivated field with rivulets running through, and herds of antelope in the distance. On through Weston Pass, I beheld and wondered and exclaimed, "Who made this, Oh God!" I can only describe it by saying it was one of Colorado's sunsets. Those who have seen them know how glorious they are. Those who have not cannot imagine anything so gorgeously beautiful. We camped on the bank of a clear stream called Jefferson Creek. I went to washing soiled clothes in the clear running creek. The men went up the stream and fished. We had broiled trout that night for supper and passed the evening over a game of whist by the light of our campfire. We wandered around in the park several days, trying to find the tracks of a party of miners that had come in over Kenosha Hill. We knew them when they left Denver. They had a packed jack. We could find no trace of them.

About the fourth day in the Park we came to Salt Creek late at night. We tried the water and found that we could not let the cattle drink from the stream. Neither could we use it ourselves. So, another night we retired hungry and thirsty. The wind blew furiously, as it invariably does in the spring of the year over the park. The night was cold, as usual, in the Park. A jack ass came to our tent door and stood in the hot embers of the campfire until he singed his ankles, and the odor that was wafted into our tent was anything but refreshing. The men drew their carbines and watched for guerrillas, and many were the conjectures as to whom he belonged. He stayed with us to the end of our trip and for many hours he carried babe and myself upon his back.

We moved on the next day to fresh water and camped on Trout Creek. Knowing that a party of men had left Denver a few days before we did, and feeling anxious to come up with them, the men shouldered their rifles and started out in search of footprints, each going in a different direction. The one who came upon the trail was to fire off his gun as a signal to the others. All day long I listened for the report of a gun. The men had not arrived when night's shadows gathered around, and I felt desolate indeed, alone with a babe, without a dog. How bitter I lamented having sent my "Patty" away. The jack came into the tent and laid down. I was even glad of his company. I laid my head down upon him and cried with loneliness. The men had gone farther than they thought before turning, and it was midnight before they found camp, and would not have found it at all but for the fire I kept burning. As they did not find the trail, we concluded to follow the way a stick might fall. It fell pointing southwest, and we went in that direction. Finding what we thought a good fording place in the Arkansas river, we decided to cross, as the road seemed better on the other side. The river was very rapid and full of boulders, around which clung cakes of ice. We found what we thought was the best fording place and drove our oxen in. Our oxen, thin, weak and tired were numb with cold, and halted in the middle of the river, and any amount of driving would not make them go. We "Whoa, Ha" and Gee Ha! but to no avail. The men plunged into the cold stream, which was waist deep, tied ropes to their horns, went upon the opposite shore and endeavored to drag them over. They were numb with cold and would not heed. The men were obliged to unload the wagon putting the goods upon the ice which was liable to break off and float away any moment; unyoke the oxen, drag the wagon over, and the oxen too. They carried the goods on their shoulders. The faithful little jack carried baby and me, although he could only keep his nose above water. We were six hours crossing the Arkansas River. We started a camp fire and dried our clothing on us, and nursed the oxen all night. We felt that we must save them, for our provisions were getting low, and we should have to eat them before long, unless game came in from the valley. We camped in this place a week or more. One man would fish, one hunt, and the other would take a pan and shovel and wash out dirt, always finding a few specks of gold to a pan of dirt. Our evenings were passed in playing cards and relating home news.

Our next move was to follow up the river. After many hard days going over steep, rocky hills we camped where Cache Creek empties into the Arkansas. Here we pitched our tent and went to work in earnest.

Mr. Tabor and Maxcy whip-sawed some boards, made two sluice boxes, sawed riffles from a log, made a ditch from the creek and commenced to wash the bank away. Cleaning the boxes up every night, we found plenty of fine gold but more black sand. Being new at mining, we knew no way to separate the gold from the sand only with the slow process of lifting the iron sand with a small magnet. Every day I would work hard trying to separate the metals and when night came I would weigh my days work and find that I had only a few pennyweights of gold. Four weeks we tarried and worked this way. Our provision was gone and we felt discouraged. It had been one long year since we heard from the loved ones at home. We were depending upon the aim of our guns for food. Our bill of fare for breakfast was;broiled venison, fried mountain sheep. Dinner; venison roast and boiled mountain mutton. Supper; fried venison, baked sheep.

One morning we saw a man coming toward camp, riding a jack. He said he was one of the party that left Denver a few days in advance of us. He seemed surprised to see a woman in camp. He told us to move on up 20 miles or more across the river, and turn up a gulch after passing a huge bald mountain. He was with a party that had found gold in paying quantities. (It was coarse and easily separated from the black sand.) At first we were doubtful, but he showed us about an ounce in small nuggets. Said that he was going out for supplies.

The next morning we left the camp and followed directions. We saw the bald mountain from the opposite side of the river and plunged in. The river looked broad and shallow. When near the opposite bank, we came into a deep channel. Our wagon bed, with myself and child in it, raised above the wheels and floated down stream. It was rapidly filling with water, when it occurred to me to cling to the willows on the bank. I did so, and held with unnatural strength until the men who were coming on the shore rescued us. I knew nothing more until we were at the mouth of California Gulch. We were three months coming from Denver, and it was the 8th day of May. We followed the stream up about six miles past the discoveries, who were down on the stream at work while we were working our way through the thick timber. The first thing after camping was to have the faithful old oxen butchered that had brought us all the way from Kansas . . . yes, from the Missouri river, three years before. We divided the beef with the miners, for they were without provisions or ammunitions.

Before night, they built me a cabin of green pine logs, without floor, door or window. I think it was 12x18 feet. The roof was covered with poles, bark and dirt. The wagon was converted into a table, side-board and three legged stools. I entered this place feeling queenly. I was happy that I once more had a roof to cover my head, and at once commenced taking boarders, with nothing to feed them except poor beef and dried apples. It was soon noised about that gold was struck in California Gulch. Before many weeks, there were ten thousand people there. A mail and express was immediately decided upon, and I was appointed Post Mistress. Letters, 76 cents each; express, equally as high, and they were kept at my cabin. Probably no other woman would be bothered with the crowd it drew. With my many duties, the days passed quickly. I also had the only gold scales in the upper part of the Gulch, where we were centrally located, so I was called upon to weigh all the gold taken from the upper part of gulch.

The miners would clean up their boxes for the day, get their gold weighed and go to town where Leadville now stands and spree all night, and return "dead broke" in the morning to commence again. During the months from May to July , I weighed $80,000 worth of gold dust that was taken out of No. 20 above Discovery for Pete Wells and Jack Langan. Our claim was No. 21 above. I had the offer of No. 20, if I would board the owner for the summer when he was in the Gulch. He wanted to run an express from Denver. Mr. Tabor was then working our mine, which was No. 12 above discovery. We took that because it had a fall, but it was a mistake, for the gold was nearly all washed over the fall into the claim below, from which $80,000 was taken out during the summer of 1860.

When September came we had cleared $4,000 from the diggings and my work. It seemed but little compared to what our neighbors had taken out. But it was so much more than we had ever had, that we were satisfied. I was very happy that summer, joyfully anticipated a visit to my mother and father in the fall. (Augusta took Maxcy with her on this trip.)

On the 20th of September, Mr. Tabor gave me one thousand dollars in dust for my visiting expenses. I packed a carpet bag with my wardrobe . . . what there was left of it, which had not been replenished since I left home. There had not been one dollar spent upon my wardrobe since I was married. Now, three years and eight months later, every dollar I had earned had gone to help make another. I took passage eastward with a mule train that was going to the Missouri river. I was five weeks crossing, and cooked for my board. This saved more money that might have been spent for travel. (The same route was used going back to Maine as was used on the first trip coming from Maine and going West.)

I will state how the $1,000 was used that was given me to go home with. As I went through Kansas, I purchased 160 acres of land adjoining, that which we already owned, for which I paid $400. In the spring I bought a pair of mules and a wagon in St Joe Missouri to return with which was $400 more. The other $200 paid my traveling expenses, and my people dressed me up. Who can say that the money was squandered? Horace joined them on their return journey to Colorado.

Mr. Tabor gave me one-fifth of what was made that summer, when I left; the other four hundred he sent to Iowa and bought flour, and in the spring we opened a store in my cabin. He worked in the mine during the day, while I attended to the store.

While we were in St Joe, Mo., buying the team and loading preparatory to another trip, the first gun was fired at Fort Sumpter. Instead of turning back and volunteering, we rushed on to get away from the war which we knew had begun. I thought of this last summer when General Logan reviewed his militia and Tabor was drawn around, dressed up in a brigadier's uniform, and was driven in front of the procession.

The spring was a cold one and I had seven in family. At Fort Kearney we were quarantined for three days, while Uncle Sam took our teams and went 80 miles into the woods for wood for the soldiers.

The Indians were numerous, and though assured that they were friendly, we were obliged to keep a watch out to keep them from driving off with our stock. They would gather around our campfire and whenever we were dining they would squat on the ground beside us, pick lice from their heads and from their children, crack them between their teeth and smile complacently at our disgust.

We were about the usual time, six weeks, crossing this time. The weather was very disagreeable. The women were cross, especially at meal time, when they would have the flapjacks and bacon nearly ready and a strong wind would scatter them over the prairie. The men, of course, were always pleasant, and why should they not be on a trip like that, when their only ambition is to lay upon the grass and play cards while the women have the wood, a scarce article to gather, the cooking and often the cattle to take care of? I do not wonder that men laugh and grow fat when they meditate how helpless women are cowed down by their iron will.

We undertook to pass the Western Range of the mountains the first of April. The snow was four feet deep upon a level and packed very solid by the winds. For many days we shoveled and worked and at last got one empty team through. Then the miners turned out en masse and opened the road for us, hearing that there were four ladies with us. There was a grand banquet prepared for us on the eve of our arrival. Hotel Booth threw wide her doors to welcome us, having had no communication with the world outside for nearly six months, with dancing, banqueting, gambling, and smoking all in the same room. The floor was puncheon, the music a fiddle, the lights tallow candles, a gambling table in each corner, where there was smoking. The wonderful supper! All it consisted of was beef, bread and dried apple sauce. There were warm hearts there, and we were very happy to see the hospitality and kind feeling that was manifested toward us by the miners.

In August, the famous Philips Lode was discovered in Park County. There was a stampede from all parts of the country, and California Gulch, being only 25 miles away across Mosquito Range, many went from there. So we, with the rest, packed up the remnants of our little store, put them into a wagon. I mounted a saddle mule, took the boy up behind and we started for the New Eldorado, bright with the hopes of doing better there.

When we were within a few miles of the top of the range, which lays between the waters of the Platte and those of the Arkansas, a fearful snow storm overtook us. We were not prepared to camp, having intended to reach the top where a man kept a toll gate. We were obliged to stop just where we were, make our bed upon three feet of snow, cover a blanket over the top and retire. Strange to say, we slept soundly and only awoke whenever the covering of snow would press to heavily upon us. When morning dawned we found that the snow under us had settled and what we had rolled from our beds during the night had formed a bank three feet high, so our bed was comfortably warm; but we could not keep it, as the oxen had been tied to the wagon without any supper, and we, too, were getting hungry. (Manuscript ends here.)

Old timers tell the author of heavy snowfalls and long winter in Leadville.

Dance House and Saloon, Leadville, Colorado.   Photo courtesy of the Colorado Historical Society.

Leadville, Colorado, July 27 1878

M. J. W. Maxwell

BOUGHT OF

H. A. W. Tabor, Dealer In

WINES. GROCERIES, PROVISIONS, LIQUORS.

MINERS' SUPPLIES.   TOBACCOS AND CIGARS.

1 Bacon   6 75

Tabor Store -- copy of a bill of sale, signed by H. A. W. Tabor, 1878.

Life in Leadville, Colorado, 1879.

Early day Leadville poker room.

Hydraulic Mining, Leadville, Colorado.

The Little Pittsburgh Mine, Leadville, Colorado.

August Rische and George Hook.   H. A. W. Tabor grubstaked these two prospectors, who discovered the Little Pittsburgh Mine.

California Gulch where Abe Lee made the first gold discovery. Horace and Augusta Tabor prospected here and at Oro, Colorado.

City of Leadville, Colorado, 1878. Sketch by J. D. Howland from the Philippe Laforgue Collection.

63

Chestnut Street, Leadville, Colorado, 1878-1879. The Tabor Bank is in the left foreground. Photo courtesy of the Oshkosh Public Museum.

Chapter Nine
The New Mining Area

A band of miners crossed over the Park Range of mountains and into California Gulch in 1860. The diggings discovered were the richest ever found and named California Gulch. Prospectors came and started the great rush. News of the discovery soon reached Denver and surrounding camps. It was not long before men from the various states made their way to the New El Dorado. In the fall of 1860, there were at least 10,000 people in the gulch. The area from Malta, at the foot of the gulch, up to Oro, at the head of the gulch, was all taken up with claims. Local miners' laws limited claims to 100 feet along the gulch. The lines extended from bank to bank.

Mining was done by means of sluices, Georgia rockers and "long Toms." The limited water supply was a great drawback to the development of the claims. Each claim owner worked diligently getting the gold out as quickly as possible.

Their dream was to work out the claim completely and return to their homes and enjoy their fortune. At this high altitude there was only about a six-months period of the year suitable for sluice mining. Huge granite boulders had to be removed, and this was a difficult task. Soon after the method of sluicing was used, the miners noticed a heavy black sand. The water just wouldn't carry off this heavy sand. Thus, it was almost impossible to separate the finer particles of gold from this sand. In fact, the sluice ways had to be shoveled out with great care so that the gold might be gathered.

Later, this despised sand was found to be almost pure silver! If only the miners had known it then.

At the close of 1865, it was thought that over three million dollars worth of silver-laden ore had been extracted from this area.

Thousands came and left during 1861-1863. So, before the discovery of silver, California Gulch was soon deserted by nearly all, except a few faithful ones like Horace and Augusta Tabor.

As previously mentioned, early in their life when conditions were so difficult, Horace had suggested that Augusta might want to go home to Maine until he had gotten established in a better way of life. She refused, saying that her place was with her husband. She loved him with all her heart and was willing to share his hard times and hope for good times in the future. Horace realized that his faithful wife would never leave him, even though conditions were not good. They were very much in love and not to be separated, and Maxcy was their pride and joy.

By 1865, the gulch mines were worked out, and in 1866 this area was deserted. A few remained along the borders, and there was a small settlement at Oro. The little hamlet of Oro was now a row of deserted and dismantled buildings, known as "Swilltown." The early miners left heaps of boulders lying around. This desolate area was not pleasant to the eye of those who followed. Those early miners came in search of gold alone and never did discover the source of this gold.

As previously mentioned, when the Tabors joined others and went on over the range to Park County, they thought their luck would be better there. At that time, they moved their store and post office and settled in Buckskin Joe. After a few years, they heard the news of a second strike in California Gulch in 1868. This was the Printer Boy Lode. Along with others, the Tabors moved back to the area of great excitement.

Oro City prospered again after the Tabors returned. The camp moved 2 1/2 miles up the gulch to reestablish near the Printer Boy Mine.

Now, Oro City #2 was an improvement over the first Oro. The best year was 1868. Great masses of almost pure gold were taken out of the Printer Boy Lode. Prospecting began again. The miners were still searching for the source of the gold. It just had to be there somewhere, if only they could find it. The Printer Boy was worked with profit for several years until it had gone down to a depth that water stopped the mining. In those days they did not have the proper machinery to continue mining with water being a problem. Still nothing had been solved about the heavy black sand.

Now our attention comes to William H. Stevens of Detroit. He had heard about California Gulch. He was familiar with several methods of hydraulic mining. Stevens felt that the gulch had not been half worked. He could see that with skilled workers the area could yield a good profit. He soon had persuaded his friend, Alvinus B. Wood, of Ann Arbor, Michigan, to join him in a venture in 1875, and a co-partnership resulted. Stevens promptly journeyed to Leadville. Plans for active operations started at once. His plan was first to wash over the tailings left by the previous miners and then work the bluff on both sides of the gulch. Hydraulic mining on a large scale began. Water from the head-waters of the Arkansas was brought via a ditch eleven miles in length. This was constructed at a cost of $50,000. The problem of the heavy sand and boulders confronted these men also. Mr. Stevens could not understand this, so consequently, he decided to investigate and make some tests. The assays convinced him it was carbonate of lead, rich in silver. They discovered it had come from the outcropping of the Rock Mine, but kept it secret. The early prospectors located and tested this mine, but pronounced it no good. It was then given up as worthless.

It was a beautiful morning in Leadville, and the Tabors had just finished breakfast. Horace and his miner friends struck out to the mines to find out about the latest developments.

Maxcy, then only eleven years of age, was a great help to his mother. Augusta beckoned him to her side and said, "Come son, let's get the store in better order." The heavier items such as sacks of flour, barrels of sugar, beans and other foodstuffs didn't need to be moved very far, only arranged in a better fashion. The move from Buckskin Joe was upsetting, but finally everything was in place and business as usual in the Tabor Store.

"Here comes the mail," exclaimed Augusta. After the mail was placed inside the store, Augusta began sorting it, ready to hand out to the anxious townspeople.

"You can finish arranging those items on the shelves, after you get the sweeping finished," said Augusta to Maxcy.

Augusta was busy weighing gold dust brought in by an early-morning customer.

Life went on, and the Printer Boy Lode caused a great deal of excitement for several years.

"If only we could locate the source of this gold," said Horace to Augusta one evening as they sat on a long bench in front of their store.

"One day it will be found," predicted Augusta, looking up the gulch with a faraway expression on her face.

Stevens and Wood were busy with their discovery. A location was first made upon the lode. They kept it all a secret. A year was spent in a careful study of the geology of the adjacent territory, particularly Rock and Iron Hill. So, these two men are credited with locating the first paying silver lode in California Gulch. They had the financial ability and technical know-how to develop their discovery. This will result in the present city of Leadville.

By 1875, Mr. Stevens, with his partner, Alvinus B. Wood, continued Hydraulic mining on a large scale.

Augusta was working long hours, tending the store and post office. She was well liked by all the people in the area. Since she knew everyone, she kept up with the news, keeping well informed.

One day the door opened and in walked William H. Stevens. "Good morning Mrs. Tabor," he greeted her with great enthusiasm. "I'd like to see Horace Tabor," he continued.

"He left early to look over the mines," answered Augusta.

"I understand that you have purchased a large area of placer ground," said Augusta.

"Yes," he nodded. "I intend to see what can be done with Hydraulic mining." "I'll be back when you are not so busy," said Mr. Stevens as he hurried out to the street.

The secret would soon be out to the public about the tests Mr. Stevens had made. He had discovered that the outcropping of the Rock Mine was the source of the silver and gold. Soon Horace and Mr. Stevens returned to the store. Horace now knew the good news and shouted, "It's the Rock Mine!" The men were laughing and slapping each other on the shoulders. Horace picked up Augusta and swung her around, as he circled the room in excitement.

This time the Tabors moved over 2 1/2 miles down the gulch and a little north to what later became Leadville.

Miners were in the habit of gathering at the Charles Mater Store. On January 18, 1878, a mass meeting of eighteen citizens met. They decided on the name of Leadville for this new town. A decision was also made to petition Governor Routt for incorporation of the town. The proclamation of the governor ordering an election was issued on January 26. On February 12, the town was formally inaugurated by election of its first Mayor, H.A.W. Tabor, and a Town Board. All were to hold office until the regular election in April.

April 3, 1878, Tabor was reelected mayor. On February 25, 1879, Governor Routt was petitioned to issue his proclamation declaring Leadville a city of first class. Tabor, as mayor, brought form and order to the rough mining town. He organized municipal law and found means for its enforcement.

Augusta was proud to have her husband in the position of Mayor and encouraged him in his political ambitions. Augusta and Horace both realized the need for a Leadville with law and order.

Mining was forging ahead rapidly.

Now we learn of Long and Derry Hill from which the J.D. Dana mine resulted. The Gallagher brothers discovered the Camp Bird and Charleston mines. Also was discovered the Carbonate Mine, after which Carbonate Hill was named. Others discovered were: Crescent, Yankee Doodle, Catalpa, Evening Star, Morning Star, and many others. 1878 was the year George Fryer dug a hole on a slight elevation directly north of Carbonate Hill.

Then with William Lovell, otherwise known as Chicken Bill, he struck the New Discovery.

One afternoon Augusta was laughing so hard that she could hardly stop. Horace had just returned from the mines. As he entered the store, he sat down on a stool near the counter. "What is so funny?" he asked.

"I'm surprised that you haven't heard this story yet," said Augusta. "It is all around town," she said, wiping her glasses on her apron. She sat down upon another stool and said, "It is about William Lovell . . . He bought some chickens with the plan of selling them in Leadville for a very high price. On his way over Mosquito Pass, he found the snow deep and the trip difficult. To add to his misery, he was caught in a blinding snow storm. He was forced to camp for the night where he was, on top of the pass. By morning he discovered his chickens were frozen. The trip took much longer than he expected, and he had no food. In a panic of hunger, he ate some of the uncooked chicken, even though partially frozen. Finally, in Leadville he did sell the chickens, so all was not lost." Ever after, his name was Chicken Bill.

Mr. Tabor had, at the opening of the carbonate excitement, two stores: one at Oro and one at Malta. The Malta store was opened in order to get the business of the first smelter located there about 1875. Population naturally drifts to a point where most advantages exist. The smelter here treated the ores from the Homestake Mine and small deposits of carbonate found in Iowa Gulch. Lack of ore was later a serious drawback and lack of business for the smelter. In 1878, the Harrison reduction works began and did a thriving business. There, population passed by Malta at the foot of California Gulch and moved up, but still not at the head of California Gulch at Oro.

Augusta and Horace had a long, serious discussion concerning the location of their store. She felt one location was enough, and that they did not need two stores. "With one store, we can have it even better stocked than before," reasoned Augusta. She, always being the practical New Englander with her frugal ways, soon had Horace agreeing with her that the location best for business was in between the two locations, the present site of Leadville. Now with the shrewdness which has characterized all her business practices, they consolidated the two stores and moved to Leadville, also taking with them the post office. The Tabor store was now a two-story brick building located at the corner of Harrison Avenue and Chestnut Street. The first business street was Chestnut and was a mile long. Harrison Avenue later took over as the Main Street, so the Tabors judged this should be a good location for business. Now the Tabor store carried the greatest stock of merchandise in the camp. Augusta felt more secure with the income from the store than from prospecting for gold.

As previously mentioned, the Tabors owned the first gold scales in the area. Augusta related how she had countless times weighed the gold for many miners.

The Tabor store also housed the first safe, and many a miner left their gold with the Tabors for safe keeping. Also, the Tabors are credited with constructing the very first brick building in Leadville, a fine two-story structure. Now, in addition to the general store, was a bank, The Bank of Leadville. Financial and Commercial needs were met by Tabor's Bank of Leadville. It was also a safe depository and medium of Exchange for Eastern capital.

Leadville could now boast of having a bank. "We really needed it," said Horace.

"Yes, and now we will not have to make those trips on horseback to Denver," commented Augusta.

Augusta recalled the days before banks when she and Horace would travel from Leadville to Denver by horseback to take gold safely there. Augusta carried some of it on her person and some in buckskins under her saddle. The express was often robbed, so this was a safe method of transportation. (They were never robbed.) In those days a woman was never molested. One story relates that Augusta hid and carried gold in her long skirts. Thus, she was known as the first bank in California Gulch and Leadville!

Chapter Ten
The Little Pittsburgh Discovery

It was spring of 1878, and August Rische and George Hook were digging a hole on the apex of Fryer Hill. The old-time miners were sure this was not the location for a mine. It definitely was not the spot in which any miner would select to prospect for gold. Hook and Rische had little experience in mining and thought one place as good as another. They were two German shoemakers from Pittsburgh. Here they were in Leadville to try their luck at mining. The experienced miners looked on and made fun of these greenhorns from the East. Rische and Hook were undisturbed by the ridicule of the experts, and they just persevered. They were grubstaked by H.A.W. Tabor.

Augusta was concerned about all the money on their books and was against any more grubstaking. Grubstake usually consists of flour, bacon, coffee, salt, tobacco, and sometimes whiskey. The prospector starts out with his burro loaded down with the necessary provisions, tools etc. Should he strike anything, he is honor-bound to share with the man who had staked him to his "grub". If he does not strike anything, he does not owe the storekeeper a cent.

Mr. Tabor took more chances in mining than any other man in the camp. The first grubstake ran out and the prospectors returned to Tabor for more. Again, this generous merchant gave a second grubstake and sent them back to work. The vein struck by Fryer in the New Discovery was supposed to dip to the east. Thus, the most moderate calculation of the depth that Rische and Hook would have to go to strike a vein would be 500 feet.

The miners crowded into the Tabor Store, not only to purchase supplies, but to talk with the Tabors. Mining activity was the main topic of the day. One day several miners were loading their burros with supplies from the Tabor Store. A lengthy conversation ensued with Horace inquiring, "Have you heard any more about August Rische and George Hook?"

"Oh, those immigrants prospecting on Fryer Hill don't know what they are doing," remarked one miner.

"They will never strike it where they are working now" added the other miner. They turned and with an abrupt exit hurried off with their burros in the direction of Fryer Hill.

Augusta listened to the end of the discussion concerning Rische and Hook. When the customers had all gone, Augusta confronted Horace and said, "I told you it was a waste of money to give Rische and Hook that grubstate. We all work hard to get ahead and, of late, too many supplies and groceries have been going for grubstakes."

Later in the day, the door flew opened, and who should appear but Rische and Hook! "We want another grubstake," yelled Rische. The first grubstake had run out and they depended on Tabor to help them again.

"Yes, I think we will have something soon," added Hook.

Augusta could hold back no longer and blurted out, "Hold on here, we can't put out any more grubstakes!"

With eyes downcast, the pair stood in silence. Horace stepped up closer to the prospectors and said quietly, "Let's give them another chance Augusta, they are hard workers."

Augusta did not say another word. She stomped out of the room and busied herself in the post office.

Again Horace was generous and gave a second grubstake. With encouraging words, he sent them back to work.

In the days ahead, business at the store kept the Tabors busy. Maxcy, 21 years of age now, knew the business well and did his share of work. Even Horace was helping wait on customers! One day he was occupied with slicing bacon for a young girl sent to the store by her mother, who was anxious to be on her way with the purchase. Outside, silence was broken by loud voices nearing the store entrance. Hilarious shouts filled the air, then, with a loud thud, the door flew open, and there stood Rische and Hook. In their hands were high-grade ore samples. They waved their arms wildly over their heads.

Everyone in the store had their attention as they announced to the Tabors that they had struck it rich! Horace was so excited after looking at the samples that he forgot to wait on his customer wanting the bacon. He rushed back to the counter and wrapped up the entire slab of bacon (partly unsliced), knife and all, and thrust the package across the counter to the young girl!

Lo and behold, to the surprise of all, mineral was uncovered at a depth of 26 or 28 feet! (Information taken from the History of the Arkansas Valley, O.L. Baskin & Co. 1881.)

This grubstake paid off, and it was named the Little Pittsburgh. According to the agreement, Hook and Rische each had a third interest, and Tabor, a third for furnishing the grubstake. Ore was mined at once, and the Little Pittsburgh was ranked as one of the leading mines in the country. During first half of July, the yield from the mine was $8,000 per week. Neighboring claims were purchased.

There is another version of the August Rische and George Hook discovery. These two prospectors were not stupid, and Rische did have some training and experience. I submit information as follows:

August Rische came to Colorado in 1868 and opened a shoe shop in Fairplay. While there he staked several prospectors, but he never made any money in these deals. In the fall of 1874, Mr. Rische came to Lake County, California Gulch and engaged in mining. He took lessons from Charley Field, S.D. Newman, and William Pierce in the Printer Boy mine. In 1875, he leased the Five-Twenty, but it was not a success. Rische began prospecting at the head of the Arkansas and discovered some valuable fissure veins. In the winter of 1877, he was prospecting on Mount Zion with George Freassle. Freassle kicked Rische's dog. This caused hot words and ended the partnership. It was a lucky kick for Rische as it placed him on the road to fortune.

On April 20, 1878, he formed a partnership with George T. Hook and was grubstaked by H.A.W Tabor. They prospected on Fryer Hill, and on May 1 discovered the Little Pittsburgh mine. They struck mineral at a depth of 26 feet.

In September, Mr. Hook sold his interest to Tabor and Rische for $90,000. According to history of Arkansas Valley, Hook sold his interest to Tabor and Rische for $140,000. He returned to his home in the East to enjoy the fruits of his good fortune. This stroke of good luck, in only a few months, brought Mr. Hook from poverty into the possession of wealth. Mr. Rische lived in great comfort, thereafter, having sold his third interest to J.B. Chaffee and David H. Moffat for $262,500.

Chapter Eleven
Tabor Luck Prevails

The Chrysolite, located at the north end of the New Discovery, was discovered by Chicken Bill Lovell. He was anxious to sell this mine, but had not yet struck pay dirt. He stole good ore from the Little Pittsburgh and salted his worthless mine, the Chrysolite. He called H.A.W. Tabor over to see his mine, showing him the good ore from Mr. Tabor's own Little Pittsburgh, which had been strewn around the Chrysolite.

Much to Chicken Bill's delight, Tabor bought the mine and had his men start work there immediately. The miners soon returned to Tabor and informed him that he had purchased a worthless mine. They had not struck mineral. Tabor told them to keep digging anyway. After sinking the shaft a little more than twenty feet, the miners struck a great bonanza. Fortune was on Tabor's side, and the swindle which Chicken Bill had intended for Tabor resulted in a great strike.

Augusta and Horace were rejoicing over the results of the purchase of the Chrysolite from Chicken Bill Lovell. A customer in the store said, "Well, Horace you were lucky again, it seems you have the King Midas touch --- everything turning to gold or silver!"

Horace was continually occupied with his mining interests. Finally, Augusta found an opportunity to talk to him about their future. "Sit down Horace, we must talk," said Augusta. "We have enough money now to live in comfort the rest of our lives," she continued. "We can save and invest our money wisely, and it will enable us to enjoy our future years happily together," said Augusta.

"I do not want to stop now," said Horace, raising his voice in protest. It was evident that Horace was caught up in the glories of wealth. After a long silence, Augusta saw that she could not convince Horace to give up the hard work and enjoy the future years together. Augusta felt she was being left behind, and it seemed useless to argue about this any further. Horace seemed a bit angry with Augusta and left the room in a huff.

Augusta was sad at the turn of events in their lives. "Alas," said Augusta to herself, "What can I do to get Horace away from all this?"

Days passed by, and Leadville was a busy city. Business at the store kept Augusta and Maxcy working long hours. Augusta had been busy nearly all day sorting the mail. Maxcy was in the store section waiting on customers. Presently, he heard his mother's voice, "Come here son and help me with the mail. I hope you can leave the store long enough to bring me the rest of the mail bags from the back room."

An anxious man stood at Augusta's side and pleaded, "Mrs. Tabor, I'm sure there is a letter for me from home, please look through it again," he continued.

"No, you will have to wait until we get the last bags sorted," answered Augusta, peering over her glasses. She glanced up long enough to see a long line of people waiting for their mail. Today the line extended way outside of the store and into the street.

The new Tabor store and post office, now located at the corner of Chestnut Street and Harrison Avenue, continued to do a thriving business. It was an ideal location because of its proximity to the Tabor home in the three hundred block on Harrison Avenue. The Tabor home was originally built where the Tabor Opera House now stands at 306-308-310 Harrison Avenue. The home was built by the Tabors about 1877, and, in 1879, Mr. Tabor wanted it moved from that location to make way for the Tabor Opera House. The new location was Carbonate Avenue, later known as East Fifth Street.

Augusta said to Horace, "I hate to have our home moved from Harrison Avenue." Horace kept insisting that it was necessary to make way for the construction of the Tabor Opera House. Augusta finally agreed, since Harrison Avenue was taking over as the business area, and that there would be no room there for homes.

This charming clapboard residence had a beautiful bay window constructed at the center-front of the building. This enhanced the luxurious parlor. As a finishing touch of elegance to the roof area, elaborate trim was added to the eaves of the entire roof.

The interior room designs were pleasing. Serviceable features were utilized in a practical way, just as Augusta directed. The home was done in fine Victorian furniture of that day. Lace curtains and other furnishings were arranged by Augusta in her own tasteful manner. The Parlor was her great pride and joy.

Augusta's kitchen had a beautiful, black cook stove. This range furnished as much heat as did the parlor heater. Cupboards, table and chairs equipped Augusta for all her kitchen work. She had beautiful dishes and silverware. Augusta could 'set a good table.' The large table had enough leaves so that it could be extended out to the desired size for any occasion. There was ample drawer space in a cabinet for all of her linens. Horace made a fine wood box with a hinged cover for Augusta, which had its place at the side of the range.

The Tabor home at 116 East Fifth Street, Leadville, Colorado. Photo courtesy of Peggy Ducharme.

Interior of the Tabor Home. The parlor. Photo by Evelyn Furman, 1992.

Ivan Laforgue at the Tabor home. On the wall above is a painting of Augusta Pierce Tabor, Ivan's great, great, great grandmother. Photo by Peggy Ducharme, 1984.

Interior of the Tabor Home. The dining room. Photo by Evelyn Furman, 1977.

Interior of the Tabor Home. The parlor. Photo by Evelyn Furman, 1992.

Interior of the Tabor Home. The bedroom. Photo by Peggy Ducharme.

Interior of the Tabor Home. A glimpse of the dining room from the parlor. Photo by Evelyn Furman, 1992.

Peggy Ducharme, right, the owner of the Tabor Home, and Evelyn Furman, 1989.

The stairway, near the front entrance, led up to the second floor. There was a spacious hallway separating the bedrooms on either side. The front bedroom facing the south was the largest, which was used by Augusta and Horace. Across from the hallway and stairway on the north was Maxcy's bedroom; also, on that side and east of Maxcy's room was another bedroom. Maxcy was twenty years of age when this house was built.

The Tabor home was considered to be roomy for that day. At this time, there were in Leadville only log cabins, small houses, or dwellings. Sagebrush and trees were being cut away to make way for the building boom.

In 1881, the home was sold to a sister of Augusta, Lucy Malvina Clark, (married Arthur C. Clark, 1861.) Malvina was two years older than Augusta, age 50, when she purchased the home. The Tabors moved to Denver in 1880 after purchasing the mansion at 17th and Broadway.

Next owner of the Leadville Tabor home was Jennie A. Lancaster. (The famous house was boarded up for years.)

When I arrived in Leadville in the 1930's, I was having some dental work done by a dentist located in the old Bank Annex building just across the street from the old Tabor home. As I sat there in the dentist chair, my attention was drawn to this old vacant house. It looked so neglected and obviously had not been painted for years. The wooden shingles were curled up and out of shape. I remarked to the dentist, "I have never seen shingles in such a curled condition."

"Do you know who once owned that house?" asked the dentist. Of course I did not know. "That was once the Tabor home," he said.

I was surprised and remarked, "Something ought to be done to preserve it." Years passed by, and finally Mrs. Dorothy Larson became interested, and the Larsons purchased it, began restoration, and opened it as a tourist attraction.

The present owner, Mrs. Peggy Ducharme, keeps the home in fine condition. She gives it her own personal touches and loving care, just as Augusta would have done.

The rooms are all beautifully done with Victorian furniture and furnishings. Bookcases, pictures and bric-a-brac, and many items of interest can still be seen today. This is the only Tabor home still in existence. All the Tabor property in Denver has been demolished.

This home was built just before the Tabors made millions in mining. They were happy then. Many relatives and friends were entertained in this home. It is said that in 1880 the Tabors entertained ex-President and Mrs. Ulysses Grant here.

When I came to Leadville, there were few people that remembered Augusta. One who reminisced about the Tabors was Frank E. Brown, who operated a grocery store at the corner of Poplar Street and East 10th Street. He told of how active Augusta was in church work and the Ladies Aid Society. She always helped others and made gifts for the children at Christmas time. He smiled as he made this remark, "When Mrs. Tabor came into my store, she always asked for brown eggs, not white."

The year of 1877 was a busy year for the Tabors. Now they were settled comfortably in their home on Harrison Avenue.

Horace had been occupied with his mining property all day and returned to the store and post office about dark. "I'm back," he announced, as he made his way to the post office side of the building. "There were so many people around all the business places, I could hardly get in my own bank," laughed Horace.

"Well," said Augusta, "there were so many teams on the streets, and people everywhere, I could hardly cross to the other side of our street. I almost got run over by the stage that went whirling around the corner."

"It's getting late, when are we going to close?" asked Maxey."

"Yes, we have had a long day, lock the door Horace," said Augusta.

About an hour later the Tabors were having their evening meal at home. Another day ended; they were all trying to relax.

"I can't believe this is the same place where we settled when we first arrived in California Gulch, Oro, and now Leadville," said Augusta.

"Yes," said Horace, "and every day more people come here."

Augusta sat down at the large, round table in the kitchen. The lamp, in the center of the table, gave a good light to the entire room. Augusta started writing a letter to the family back home in Maine.

> *My dear ones,*
> *In the space of a year, Leadville has grown so much that we can hardly believe it, let alone describe it to you folks at home!*
> *It is early evening as I write this. There are so many people here day and night. I don't think they ever go to bed. I can hear a band going down Harrison Avenue now, playing music so loud that it is impossible to carry on a conversation and be heard, even in the house. They are advertising the shows on Chestnut and Second Streets. Gambling houses and saloons are full. Many miners spend all they make during the day in these dens of iniquity. One miner gave me his gold dust to keep for him. I put it in our safe, and last night in the middle of the night he was pounding on our door, wanted his bag of gold dust. Before morning it was gone. Every day he repeats this way of life, so he is always broke until he can earn another bag of gold dust.*

82

During the day it is noisy too, because of all the building being done. The sound of the hammer is never ending.
I look for some of you to come out for a visit soon.
Love, Gusta

H.A.W. Tabor bought and developed many more mining properties. He purchased the Matchless Mine for $117,000, a great silver producer.

In November, the New Discovery, Little Pittsburgh, Dunes and Winnemuc properties were merged into the Little Pittsburgh Consolidated Company. Afterwards, Mr. Tabor sold his interest to his partners for $1,000,000.

After this wonderful discovery, claims were staked out all over Fryer Hill. The Chrysolite and Carboniferous, Amie Dunkin, Matchless and Robert E. Lee began producing. The value of Carbonate rocks and black sand was now established.

Tabor Opera House, Leadville, Colorado. At the right is the catwalk connection to the third floor of the Clarendon Hotel. Photo courtesy of the Denver Public Library Western History Collection.

Leadville, Colorado, street scene on Harrison Avenue. The Tabor Opera House is at the right.

Leonard Shaft of the Matchless Mine, Leadville, Colorado.

Interior of the Tabor Opera House in Leadville, Colorado. The stage front curtain. Photo by Carl Schafer, 1987.

85

Chapter Twelve
Leadville Grows

Not only was Leadville a great mining area, but an interesting town in other respects, which must be considered.

The town of Leadville is beautifully situated on the western slope of Ball Mountain, one of the highest peaks of Mosquito Range. It is about two miles from the Arkansas River and directly opposite Mount Massive. The town was well laid out with streets crossing at right angles. In the early days the Arkansas River supplied all the water needed. The water was brought many miles by ditches, and small mountain streams flowed along each side of the city, swelling the water supply also.

By 1878 the growth of Leadville was so great that a system of water works had to be built. H.A.W. Tabor was chief promoter of this system. Leadville then had an ample supply of pure drinking water and for other purposes, such as fire fighting. Tabor established the Tabor Hose Company. He gave a $1200 carriage and 1250 feet of reeled hose.

Leadville's elevation is 10,152 feet above sea level, a two-mile high city.

On July 1, 1879, there were at least 20,000 people in Leadville. Buildings sprang up like magic. Business houses, hotels, banks, churches, and dwellings, all were constructed as fast as workmen could build them. The sound of the hammer of the workmen almost never ended, night or day. Areas of pine forests were seen one month, and the next month all was transformed into streets of traffic with cabins and frame dwellings in various stages of construction. People came flocking into this new El Dorado from all parts of the union, as many as one hundred per day.

The mines in 1877 changed hands for a few thousand dollars, but by 1879 they sold for millions. Town lots once sold for $25 in the spring of 1878, but by summer of 1879, they sold for $5,000. Many real estate operators became rich.

Leadville, by daylight, was a sight to behold. All classes of humanity had moved into town. Streets were filled with teams. Chestnut Street and Harrison Avenue were the main streets where tides of humanity flow. Often, at banks, men stood in long rows waiting their turn to deposit rolls of greenbacks or checks. There was an endless stream of people coming and going from the post office . . . all were hoping for a letter from home.

Groups of men congregated around the town, sitting on benches, talking excitedly about mining. Saloons were crowded with miners discussing the events of the day, especially new-mine discoveries.

Leadville, by gaslight, was even more wonderful to behold. In the evening there appeared an army of miners, speculators and capitalists. They had all returned from their work and the streets were crowded from curb to curb. No teams to be seen now, as most were all in the barns for the night. The teamsters are out for "a lark." With so many people about, the streets are fairly alive with excitement.

Pedestrians, wanting to reach any certain place in a hurry, chose the middle of the street rather than the sidewalk. Here, they took chances of being run over by the dashing horsemen and coaches always on the streets. They whirled over the smooth roadways at any hour of the day or night.

The miners are swarming in to "take in the sights." During the day, handbills have been scattered all over the town, advertising the shows at the theaters and variety houses. The bands are out helping to drum up an audience. The bands play so loudly that no one in town could sleep, even if they wanted to. The saloons are full, and painted-faced women are running here and there, waiting on the tables, carrying trays of beer and liquors. It is said that just one saloon often took in $500 in one evening.

Gambling houses run full blast, and the old adage of "easy come, easy go," holds true in these dens of infamy and hot beds of crime. The level of society in Leadville was not all low-class, but this element did predominate. Later, Leadville settled down. A better class of people came in and took up residence in permanent homes. The elements that make up a higher social life increased.

In the beginning of Leadville, there was much crime and vice. At night one could not ride out three miles from the center of town without being in danger, as one could be struck by a stray shot from a gun intended for someone else.

New mines were opened daily, and purchasers for "holes in the ground," that only gave promise of reaching mineral, were readily found. The beggar of one day became the millionaire of the next. The "tenderfoot," fresh from the states, was as likely to be successful as the experienced miner, who for years had trudged over the hills, not knowing he was walking over a fortune. In 1876 there were a few small slab cabins, but 1879, a well and substantially built city, having brick blocks, well laid-out streets, water works, gas works, opera house, daily newspapers, banks and all the businesses that make up great cities, prospered. Its voting population already outnumbered that of Denver.

Newspapers were established in Leadville. Leadville had one more daily paper than Denver!

The best mines were located within a radius of four miles from the heart of the city and are easily accessible. A short distance away are the reduction works where all the ore is reduced to bullion.

Fryer Hill was so named in honor of the man who discovered one of the most valuable mines about the camp. The New Discovery is one of the lowest ranges of hills surrounding the city and lies about one mile to the northeast of the center of the town. Up this hill are found the mines which have made the name of Leadville famous: The Little Pittsburgh, New Discovery, Winnemuc, Little Chief, Chrysolite, Little Ella, Dives, Vulture, Carboniferous, Robert E. Lee, Climax, Duncan, Matchless and many others. Leadville was well supplied with smelters, which were kept running night and day. The fires in the furnaces never being extinguished except for repairs. Those smelters gave employment to about 1,000 men. Four lines of concord coaches, each coach capable of bringing from 18 to 20 passengers, and each line having from two- to four- coaches going each way daily, ran between the cars and the city. The railroad had reached Webster, at the foot of Kenosha Hill, and was making preparations to transfer the track over the divide between Platte and South Park. Another line of coaches ran between Canon City and Leadville. By the end of the year, the population was 18,000.

Chapter Thirteen
The Tabors Build

H.A.W. Tabor set out to build Leadville into a great city. His words were: "I am going to make Leadville into a first-class city so people will want to stay here."

The Tabors started this building trend, and as more brick buildings appeared, Leadville did take on the look of a first-class city. We have learned how he promoted the water works and the fire department; also, to his credit, was the Tabor Light Cavalry, which had a body of fifty men, which was equipped at a cost of $10,000.

Another Tabor enterprise was the Tabor Milling Company, in which he invested $100,000. The city now was only two years old. In 1879, Tabor built the Tabor Opera House, with it entirely completed in just 100 days, with J. Thomas Roberts as the contractor. Roberts came to Colorado in 1870 and to Leadville in 1879. He was one of the oldest and most reliable builders in the city. He also built the Clarendon Hotel, which opened April 10, 1879. William Bush owned the Clarendon, and Tabor, his partner, helped with the financing of its construction.

At this time, only one house stood on the east side of Harrison Avenue, and only two or three on the west side of the street. It was predicted that the Clarendon and the Tabor Opera House would be business failures because their location was simply too far from Chestnut Street, then the main street of the thriving new mountain city. One man said, "What is Mr. Tabor doing . . . building way out here in the sage brush?" Before mid-year, results proved the wisdom of the location. Harrison Avenue became Leadville's prosperous main street. The Opera House was the most beautiful brick structure in Leadville.

At first, Augusta was overwhelmed at even the thought of an opera house. It seemed Horace was plunging ahead without learning Augusta's thoughts on such a great undertaking of this massive building. She was also concerned about the tremendous cost. Horace was determined to build up Leadville! Augusta, later, had second thoughts about her husband's great ambitions. "Perhaps I might as well go along with his ideas," said Augusta to Maxcy one day.

"I do not like the cheap saloons and dance halls," she continued. "At least now the opera house will have the legitimate stage where respectable people will want to go," she added. Culture was brought to Leadville by the Tabors. The Leadville people were delighted and could hardly wait for the completion of this wonderful opera house, the best west of the Mississippi!

Augusta was enjoying the company of the better class of people now arriving in Leadville. "I am happy to have relatives and friends from the East locating here. We are all having delightful times together," said Augusta.

The Tabor Opera House opened November 20, 1879. There was a covered walkway known as the "catwalk" connecting the third floor of the Tabor Opera house with the Clarendon. It extended over St. Louis Avenue and was a convenience during the inclement weather.

The building was constructed of stone, brick and iron, and trimmed with Portland cement. The frontage measures 60 feet, the length extends 150 feet, and the height reaches 60 feet. There were two spacious store sections on each side of the front entrance. The north section was occupied by Sands Pelton & Co., and the section on the south was a drug store, J.S. Miller. In the rear was Phil Goldings Saloon.

The auditorium is large and convenient; the seating was 880. Andrews' patent opera chairs of Victorian design are ornate cast iron, upholstered in red velvet. The stage is large enough to accommodate the best and greatest of productions. The color scheme in the theater is red, gold, white, and a bit of blue. There are ten sets of scenery still to be seen in this famous opera house. The cost of the building was about $78,000, not including furnishings, seats, or scenery. The front curtain cost $1,000.

The Tabor suite was on the second floor. The interior was elaborate and beautiful. It consisted of five rooms across the front of the building. Over the entrance is an elaborate sign --- TABOR SUITE.

Upon entering through the large double doors, one is impressed with the huge front windows. The height extends from the top of the wall, at the ceiling, almost to the floor. The floor-length velvet drapes are trimmed with gold fringe and caught up and draped back gracefully with gold matching cords, complete with tassels. Handmade lace curtains complete the window arrangements.

The high ceilings add to the spacious appearance of this luxurious suite. The carpeting was of the very best quality, and the pattern blended with the furnishings. The massive and costly furniture was chiefly of Victorian design. Some pieces of furniture and paintings were imported from other countries. Horace Tabor and Bill Bush each had offices in the suite. (These luxurious offices replaced those in Tabor's bank.)

When attending shows, Mr. Tabor did not always occupy the Tabor Box. On occasion, he would reserve the entire balcony and invite his guests to join him there for the shows. These theater parties overflowed to the Tabor suite, where refreshments were served all evening long.

Being that the Tabor Suite and balcony are on the same level of the second floor, there is easy access to either through doors.

Augusta wasn't too interested in the Tabor suite as a permanent living quarters; however, she did help Horace select the furnishings.

Plans were already underway for the Tabors to move to Denver. They purchased the mansion at 17th Street and Broadway. There were plans on the drawing board for more buildings in the Queen City. Horace's involvement in politics necessitated the move to Denver. The Tabors, including Maxcy, occupied the suite on visits to Leadville.

The Tabor Opera House is still standing and is owned by Evelyn Livingston Furman. Tours are available each summer season. Carl and Donna Schaeffer are in charge of melodrama during the summer. (Inquire locally for dates.)

H.A.W. Tabor built the Leadville Gas Company at a total cost of $75,000. The first building in Leadville to be lighted by gas was the Tabor Opera House; next, the city was lighted by gas.

H.A.W. Tabor donated to churches, schools, hospitals, and to any worthy cause. His average donations amounted to at least $10,000 per year.

Other accomplishments were: In 1879 the Telephone Exchange was organized with H.A.W. Tabor as President; he also owned a newspaper; and helped with the construction of the Tabor Grand Hotel. (It was first known as the Kitchen Brothers Hotel.) The owners ran out of money and then asked Mr. Tabor for financial assistance. He then completed the building, and it was named after him.

The log house, once the abode of the Tabors, is gone. The Tabor home still stands at 116 East Fifth Street, where Peggy Ducharme is the owner. It is a tourist attraction, open daily all year long for tours.

(Space in this book is limited so I do not tell of all the H.A.W. Tabor business ventures.) However, one of my favorite spots is Evergreen Lakes. I am describing this business venture where Horace made another investment, because I have found two rare photographs of the Tabors and Pierces taken on Evergreen Lakes. These photos are evidence of the happy occasions had at that time.

Tabor stamp mill. Photo courtesy of the State Historical Society of Colorado.

Lobby of the Vendome Hotel -- Tabor Grand, as it was in 1933 when the author lived there. Photo courtesy of the State Historical Society of Colorado.

This 1911 cutter is typical of winter travel in early Leadville, Colorado.

Evergreen Lake near Leadville, Colorado.

A scene at Evergreen Lake, near Leadville, Colorado. Photo courtesy of the Colorado Historical Society.

Augusta Tabor, pictured here next to H. A. W. Tabor, on the right. This is a favorite likeness to our heroine, as she is shown in her youth and beauty, smiling pleasantly. Right to left: H. A. W. Tabor; Augusta Pierce Tabor; Augusta's two brothers, the Pierces, and their wives; Mrs. Lee Pierce Taylor is seated in the front. An enlargement of Augusta in this photograph appears on the front cover of the book. Photo courtesy of the Amon Carter Museum.

H.A.W. Tabor and Augusta Pierce Tabor, at the left, and the Pierce boys and their wives at Upper Evergreen Lake. Mazzulla collection; courtesy of the Amon Carter Museum.

96

Chapter Fourteen
Evergreen Lakes

From the newspaper files of the <u>Leadville</u> <u>Herald</u> in 1879 :

The articles of incorporation of the Evergreen Lakes and Mineral Springs company were filed with recorder Wells yesterday. The objects for which the company is created are the improvement and development of such property, personal or real as may be purchased or otherwise acquired by the company, and the construction and improvement of lakes and waterworks, the propagation of fish and the erection of hotels and other building conducive to the interests of the company. The capital stock of the company is to be $100,000 to be divided into 2000 shares, of the par value of $50 each. The principal places of business will be at Leadville, Evergreen Lakes and Mineral Springs, with an office at the former and later named places. The incorporators are H.A.W. Tabor, A.S. Cooper, R.E. Goodell, J.W. Virgin and I. Wilson.

At Evergreen Lakes new facilities for the enjoyment of pleasure seekers were a new hotel, additional pleasure and fishing boats and a new road. The hotel financially backed by such Leadville men as R.E. Goodell and Dr. John Law. The hotel was located on a knoll between the second and third lakes and overlooked all three lakes. Colonel Goodell and M.G. De Mary were the promoters and builders of the new road which extended from the western end of the boulevard at Soda Springs around the base of Mount Massive to Evergreen Lakes and on to Malta. Here it joined the old road to Leadville. This roadway was known as The Circle Drive, and later also as The Loop.

The Boulevard section of the road ran west from the foot of west Third street to the race track, Soda Springs and the Mount Massive Hotel.

On July 4th 1882 about two thousand people gathered at Evergreen lakes to enjoy the rustic place. There is no prettier spot anywhere in the area. Preparations had been made for a general good time and lots of fun. Bright painted boats were moored on the granite banks of the mountain lakes. A large platform had been erected for those wanting to dance, and a well selected orchestra was engaged. The barbecue, under the auspices of the Tabor light cavalry was a genuine success. The aroma of the roast beef gave everyone a great appetite. It was devoured in a short time.

Augusta and Horace circulated through the crowd, beaming with pleasure as they were greeted by Leadville people. There were many hand shakes as the Tabors were thanked for this wonderful place of amusement, and for the abundance of delicious food! One of the finest boulevards conceivable leads to Evergreen lakes. This beautiful road is from six to seven miles long about 100 feet wide. It is as smooth as an oiled ballroom floor. Before reaching Evergreen Lakes one comes to Soda Springs, a pleasant and convenient stopping place. Evergreen Lakes lie at the foot of Mt. Massive. Now one of the grandest sights to behold anywhere comes into view. Far beyond the picturesque valley of the Arkansas lies Leadville at the foot of Mosquito Pass.

The Tabors, their relatives and friends continued to enjoy leisure time at Evergreen Lakes. Augusta and Horace liked to entertain groups and occasionally stayed at the hotel. (Note photographs shown in this book of Augusta, Horace, Augusta's two brothers and wives; also a sister, Lilla, Mrs. C.F. Taylor.)

Eating at the hotel was enjoyed, as the food was delicious. On this occasion, the Tabors and Pierces spent a few days at the hotel. They all enjoyed boating, as evidenced by the photograph.

"I have really enjoyed fishing, especially toward evening," said Augusta's brother.

"We will fish as often as you like," said Horace.

On the return trip to Leadville, all were happy and relaxed. "I can't wait to go again," remarked Lilla to Augusta.

As mentioned previously, today the lakes are now used by the National Fish Hatchery. The hotel is gone. The beautiful boulevard, a thing of the past, but the road still exists, and one can drive around the loop, stopping at Soda Springs. The water is available to anyone. Some take home jugs of this water and add lemon juice, making an interesting drink. Others declare that they receive health benefits from drinking this soda water .

According to clippings of the <u>Rocky Mountain News,</u> in June and August of 1879, the Tabors entertained relatives of Augusta at Soda Springs near Evergreen Lake. Today, Evergreen Lakes is still one of the more scenic spots in the Leadville area. It is the rearing ponds of the National Fish Hatchery.

Tabor Grand Opera House, Denver, Colorado. Photo courtesy of the Library of the State Historical Society of Colorado Collection.

Detail of an oil painting on canvas, attached to the plastered wall of the Tabor Bar in the Windsor Hotel, Denver, Colorado. H.A.W. Tabor is at the left. Original painting from the collection of Evelyn Furman.

99

Mansion of Augusta Tabor at 17th and Broadway, Denver, Colorado. Photo courtesy of the Library of the State Historical Society of Colorado Collection.

Brown Palace Hotel, Denver, Colorado. Residence of Augusta Tabor after she moved from the mansion on 17th and Broadway.

H.A.W. Tabor, great grandfather of Philippe Laforgue.

*Augusta Pierce Tabor, great grandmother of Philippe Laforgue.   Photo
courtesy of the Philippe Laforgue Collection.*

H.A.W. Tabor. Photo given to the author by David R. McCurry. Photo originally from Emily Jane Tabor Moyes, the sister of H.A.W. Tabor and great, great grandmother of David R. McCurry.

"Augusta Pierce Tabor, first wife of H.A.W. Tabor" is the caption on the back of the original photo from the Emily Jane Tabor Moyes collection. *This rare and excellent photo has never before been published. Photo given to the author by David R. McCurry.*

The home of Maxcy and Luella Tabor, 1120 Grant Street, Denver, Colorado. Luella's three brothers, Charles, Frank and John Babcock, also lived here. Luella's sister, Persis Gray, lived in San Francisco, California. None had children except Luella whose daughter, Persis Augusta Tabor, was the mother of Philippe Laforgue.

Nathaniel Maxcy Tabor, father of Persis Augusta Tabor and grandfather of Philippe Laforgue.

Luella Babcock Tabor, wife of Maxcy Tabor, mother of Persis Augusta Tabor and grandmother of Philippe Laforgue.

Persis Augusta Tabor Laforgue, mother of Jacques Philippe Laforgue. Born May 29, 1894, at the Brown Palace Hotel, Denver, Colorado. Died January 28, 1981, in Palena Mallorca, Spain.

Paul Alain Laforgue, father of Jacques Philippe Laforgue. Born in Santa Rosalia, Baja California, Mexico, April 17, 1889. Died August 24, 1938, in Paris, France. Married Persis Augusta Tabor on February 24, 1914, in Denver, Colorado.

Chapter Fifteen
Tabor Builds In Denver

Fame of the Tabor riches had gone abroad far and wide. Augusta, his faithful wife, remained by his side. They labored long and hard before reaping the reward they so richly deserved.

Many of the early miners gave up in their search for gold, but Horace Tabor was adventurous and had faith in the "Star of Silver" shining so brightly over the hills. He invested thousands and reaped millions!

After the arrival of the railways, people flocked to Colorado. Many were from Eastern United States. Trips west were now pleasure excursions instead of the rough journey of the past. Many came suffering from tuberculosis. Living in Colorado, they were cured. They took up residence here and began careers of usefulness in this state. It was soon discovered that they must remain here to keep in good health; the dry and rarefied air of Colorado was a cure.

Leadville is noted for its blue, cloudless skies. There is limited rainfall in this state, and the sun shines about 300 days out of every year.

There was once a restaurant owner in Leadville that offered a free meal to anyone coming in to claim it on any day when the sun did not shine some part of the day. Under these conditions, there were very few free meals.

With Leadville's rise to fame came Denver's prosperity. Money made in Leadville mining built up Denver.

Mr. Tabor invested in buildings and real estate in Denver, causing prices to rise. Houses doubled in price, building materials, such as brick and lumber, became scarce and expensive. Wages of working men, especially carpenters and masons, rose to high figures.

The Tabor Block was another venture built in the spring of 1880. It was constructed of sandstone cut at Cloughs' quarries in Ohio. The fronts were of gray-colored stone. It was a five-story brick with Munsard roof. Elevators and all the modern improvements that add to its comfort and security were installed. The building and ground cost Tabor $200,000. This business building was a great asset to Denver and insured a good income for the builder.

In 1880, Mr. Tabor purchased the corner of Sixteenth and Curtis Streets. There he built the Tabor Grande Opera House. A Chicago firm drew up the plans. Mr. Tabor gave them instructions to visit the best theaters in America and Europe. After those inspections, they were to erect a building that would equal or surpass the finest in the country. The Tabor Grand Opera House cost $200,000. It had beauty of design, elegant finish, and acoustic properties not surpassed by any other east or west.

On September 5, 1881, it was opened to the public by Emma Abbotts Company.

Governor Tabor bought 890 of the 2,000 shares of the First National Bank of Denver, where he was vice president .

Tabor bought the corner of Arapahoe and Sixteenth Street and gave it to the government as a site for a post office, which was later erected there.

In 1878, Mr. Tabor was elected lieutenant governor of Colorado. He now was occupied with business ventures and politics in Denver. Horace Tabor saw that Denver was a fruitful field of operation, and he began to build.

Mr. Tabor purchased the H.C. Brown residence and the spacious grounds covering an entire block. The cost was $40,000, and he later spent $20,000 more on improvements. This mansion, in the center of the city, is located on a picturesque site, with a fine view of the mountains.

When Tabor proudly escorted Augusta to the Brown mansion, (home of the builder of the Brown Palace Hotel) she said, "I will never go up these steps, Tabor, if you think I'll have to come down them." Was she thinking of the ups and downs of their lives in searching for gold?

From The Denver Daily
February 8, 1879

Mr. Tabor At Home
Splendid Success of the Reception Given by the Lieutenant-Governor Who Were Present to Enjoy the Affair

———————

Governor and Mrs. Tabor threw wide the doors of their mansion last evening, and extended the hospitalities of his house to the members of the General Assembly and many other guests.

It is already quite generally known that he purchased the residence of H.C. Brown, and last evening the place was filled to overflowing with the many friends of the new Lieutenant-Governor.

Governor Tabor and his estimable lady received the many friends who presented themselves, and welcomed all with the bidding that they make themselves at home and take possession of the house. The preparations had been thorough and elegant. One of the parlors was especially prepared for the devotees of Terpsichore, and during the whole evening beautiful and enticing music urged and attracted those who love to dance. No better invitation was needed, and the parlor was full of happy faces.

The full suite of rooms on the opposite side of the hall was thrown open and in the first the host and his lady sat entertaining their visitors; scattered through and all over the rooms were groups of ladies and gentlemen. Truly, "The lights shone o'er fair women and brave men."

On the upper floor was the wine room, which by its attractions drew visitors constantly, who were fully served with anything that heart could wish, and that of a quality beyond criticism. Those who smoked, and connoisseurs sipped and praised the wines of their generous host.

Passing again to the lower floors the guests found a collation laid for their further entertainment. A beautiful pyramid in the center of the table was the first object to attract the eye . . . no, not the first, for the pleased countenances of the many guests, both of the gentler and the sterner sex, gathered about the board were the first to attract attention. But the pyramid was beautiful and every appointment of the festive board was in keeping with its elegance. Besides there were side tables at which tete a tetes were held and which seemed not less attractive than the more extensive spread.

A varied collection of the substantial things of life was served together with a full supply of the choicest articles of dessert. Tunnell & Co. made a special effort on this occasion and their success is worthy of the highest commendation. A numerous corps of attendants assured the fact that each guest should be attended in a manner corresponding with the expressed intention of the host and hostess.

The guests arrived constantly until a late hour and yet there was always room and a hearty welcome.

Many of the guests were scattered over the house enjoying the good things of life, and the pleasure of a quiet talk, while as many more indulged in the more lively amusements. The combined effect of the perfect ease at which the guests felt themselves, the music, the brilliant light and the abundant good cheer served to render it an occasion of through enjoyment. We venture to say that there has not for many a day been an occasion at all approaching it in success and éclat. The guests were not in full dress but were made comfortable without the studied ceremony which burdens many gatherings.

Among the guests assembled were many gentlemen and ladies well known to the people of Denver:

Attorney General Wright and lady.

Representative T.J. Cantlon, of Clear Creek.

Representative Toll, of Rio Grande.

Representative Clark, of Las Animas.

Senator Helm, of El Paso.

Senator DeFrance, of Jefferson.

Representative Luthe, of Arapahoe.

Mr. Streeter, Speaker of the House.

Senator E.O. Wolcott, of Clear Creek.

Representative Trujillo, of Costilla.

Representative Maez.

Representative Todd, of Arapahoe.

Senator Haynes, of Weld.

Senator Rhodes, of Larimer.

Senator Neikirk, of Boulder.

Representative Voorhies, of San Juan and Ouray.

Representative Evans, of Boulder.

Representative Thomas, of Pueblo.

Judge W.B. Felton, clerk of the House, and Messrs. Maxwell, Scott, Bingham, Brandt, Valdez, Salazar, Vigil and Pease, all solons of the present session.

General Judd Brush, Representative from Weld, was also in attendance. Among the members of the State executive were Hon. J.C. Shattuck, State Superintendent of Public Instruction, and State Auditor Stimson. The last executive corps was ably represented by ex-Secretary of State Wm. M. Clark and ex-Governor Routt. Senator Hill was also among the guests.

Prominent among the laymen were Captain W. R. Bradley of Georgetown, Colonel Archer, Mr. D.E. Parks, a prominent lawyer of Leadville, and Wolfe Londoner. Surveyor General Campbell and lady were also among those gathered to do honor to the host and hostess.

The fair sex was not less fully nor less fittingly represented and added, as they always do, greatly to the pleasure of the occasion. Among them were Mrs. Governor Routt, Mrs. Senator Hill, Mrs. Rogers, Mrs. Tallant, Miss Hood, Miss Overton, Miss Anthony, Mrs. General Cameron, Mrs. J.C. Shattuck, Miss Florence Haynes and Miss Jennie Cameron.

These and many other guests made up a gathering among which "all went merry as a marriage bell."

Plants and flowers tastefully arranged and distributed added to the beauty of the spacious parlors.

The affair was a success on which Governor Tabor and his wife are to be congratulated and which their many friends will always remember with pleasure.

Mrs. Tabor adjusted to her new position in society easily. In her first reception in Denver given to the Legislature she was assisted by Mrs. Governor Rautt. She was a graceful, well-trained woman and had been in Washington society for several seasons. However, both ladies were equally at home in their duties.

Mrs. Tabor appeared in a simple, black silk, piped with canary and wore a diamond cross. Several old ladies were present. They were not in society but had been Mrs. Tabor's friends in former years. Mrs. Tabor did not ignore them for newer or more elegant ones. Mrs. Tabor was criticized because she allowed her servants to come into an adjoining room and listen to the music. Mrs. Tabor always welcomed her old friends, miners, and poor people. She never did slight any of them.

Horace continues spending money lavishly. Augusta thought he was wasting huge sums and was too extravagant. Mr. Tabor's carriage cost $2,000 and is a facsimile of the one belonging to the White House. Augusta once said , "If we had only had the money that is in that carriage when we began life!"

Augusta was proud to have been a pioneer woman and related how she and her husband helped found Leadville and build up that city; also Denver. She was the first white woman in California Gulch, and she stated that there would be no Leadville today if her husband had not stayed in the gulch and persevered in keeping store for the miners. She indignantly denied that Governor Tabor was very poor when the Little Pittsburgh was discovered and stated that his store was valued at $25,000.

Her version of the discovery of carbonate is that Mr. Stevens of Stevens and Leiter, of the Iron Mine, first told them that while digging for gold, they were walking over silver. No one of that time realized the extent and value there.

A newspaper article once contained a sneering account that stated: "Mrs. Tabor's New England grammar, (If there is such a thing as sectional and New England grammar) is also the grammar of Emerson and others, as she is very strict and choice in her language."

She has corresponded at different times for Eastern papers. She and a newspaper reporter, a friend, attended a meeting of the State Press Association in Manitou, Colorado, July 13, 1879. Augusta kept a journal on the way that showed keen observation and ability to compose a better report than other newspaper reporters to send to their respective papers.

July 13, 1879, the following article appeared in the <u>Rocky</u> <u>Mt</u>. <u>News</u>:

"At the ball at Manitou house, ladies of the press club party wore some very pretty costumes. Mrs. Governor Tabor wore black silk with diamond jewelry."

Various churches were seeking the newly-rich Tabors' memberships. Augusta remarked, "I suppose Mr. Tabor's and my souls are of more value than they were a year ago."

Augusta was still an attractive woman. She was a thin person, rather angular, with curling dark hair. She wears blue glasses to benefit her near-sighted eyes. Her voice is especially soft and pleasant. Contrary to the opinion of some, she was well dressed. She had good taste in dress, usually wearing subdued, but not somber colors.

<u>Augusta's</u> <u>scrapbook</u>: 1/1/1881

"A brilliant reception at New Years mentioned the guests and how they were dressed. Mrs. Tabor . . . Cream embossed satin and point lace: ornaments diamonds and fresh cardinal flowers."

<u>From</u> <u>Augusta</u> <u>Tabor's</u> <u>scrapbook</u>: "April 4, 1881, Mrs. H.A.W. Tabor will leave in a few days for the east, enroute to Europe."

Augusta was once asked if her son should marry someone she did not approve of what would she do about that. Augusta answered "I would try to like her, because he liked her." If all women, in this respect, were only like Mrs. Tabor.

Members of Augusta's family came from Maine and began investing in Leadville and Denver. Some stayed with Augusta in the Broadway Mansion, as did boarders.

Horace resented Augusta's criticism of his being a big spender. Her frugal ways irritated him. Augusta, too, liked nice things and wore lovely clothes and jewelry. However, she felt that Horace was going to extremes in unncessary purchases. She disliked his show-off nature. He complained of her nagging ways. Wealth did not seem to bring true or lasting happiness to the Tabors.

Augusta felt left out in Horace's business activities. He had employed experienced men to handle his business affairs. As Horace became involved with greater enterprises, he did not discuss these business ventures with Augusta, as he once did. Maxcy, now a young man, helped his father in some of the businesses. Augusta was delighted with the beautiful mansion, but concerned about Horace drifting away from her.

In 1880 Horace and Augusta continued to drift apart. By January 1881, Horace decided on a permanent move from the Broadway mansion and left Augusta forever.

Business took Horace around the country most of the time. When not traveling, the Windsor Hotel served as his headquarters. The Windsor, a very plush hostelry, opened in June 1880. Horace Tabor and William Bush invested in this magnificent building. Records reveal that Charles L. Hall owned a one-third interest in the Windsor. He sold his interest to Mrs. H.A.W. Tabor. Both Horace Tabor and William Bush were irritated by Augusta's ownership of interest in the hotel. Finally, Horace managed to get Bush to act as a front to purchase Augusta's interest in the building.

Why did Augusta purchase a third interest in the Windsor? It was a good investment, and in addition to that, it was a chance for her to check up on Horace and his affairs. She was seen strolling through the halls and sitting in the lobby visiting with friends. This was an awkward situation for Horace and caused him untold embarrassment.

Horace was occupied with the construction of the Tabor Grand Opera House in Denver. At this time, Augusta and Horace were not divorced, but estranged.

Chapter Sixteen
Enter Baby Doe . . . Augusta's Darkest Hour

Now, that we have the Tabors at this point, there comes a turn of events that changed the Tabor story. It became whispered about that Mr. Tabor was paying attention to a young woman, beautiful and dashing, whom the facetious nick-named Baby Doe. Enter Elizabeth Mc Court Doe!

There exists some controversy as to when and where Horace Tabor met this beautiful blue-eyed blonde. She was a divorcee. She and her husband, Harvey Doe, had come west from Oshkosh, Wisconsin, to Central City. They were accompanied by Harvey's parents. The elder Does had mining interests in Central City and had come to seek their fortune there. Harvey Doe was not successful with the mining venture, and after a few years, his wife became dissatisfied and divorced him.

Peter Mc Court, brother of Baby Doe, came to Colorado in 1873, lured by the territories' mining boom. Mc Court met Tabor in Leadville. Close association between the two men resulted in business connections later. It is possible that Horace might have met Baby Doe some years before she appeared in Leadville. Both men, having mining interests, congregated with the mining men of Denver. So, Horace may have met Baby Doe in Denver, or even in New York.

It is evident that Elizabeth McCourt Doe was aware of H.A.W. Tabor and his millions. People all around the world were fascinated by the Tabor story. Newspapers carried accounts of his success.

Business had dropped off in Central City, but was booming in Leadville. Mrs. Doe had previously taken up with Jacob Sandelowsky or Jacob Sands, as he was called. He owned a men's clothing store in Central City. She accompanied this friend when he moved with his business to Leadville. Soon Mrs. Doe, who had been nicknamed Baby Doe while in Central City, met Horace Tabor. Greatly attracted to each other, a love affair followed.

Horace wanted to marry Baby Doe. Next, he was plotting and planning for a divorce. Augusta was not at all willing, as she loved her husband and wanted to keep him. After all, a divorce was a disgrace in that day.

The matrimonial problems of Augusta and Horace were now in the open. Augusta was crushed to think that her husband would cast her aside for a younger, beautiful divorcee. What a change had come over Horace! Augusta spent sleepless nights trying to decide on a solution to this terrible turn of events.

It was humiliating to think of her husband with another woman. Since a divorce was a scandal in that day, what would her relatives and friends think? Augusta's world was falling apart. She had been the frugal one and had held everything together financially. She had always disapproved of her husband's extravagance of expenditures on furniture, expensive carriages, diamond shirt studs and other jewelry.

Augusta feared Horace would soon be financially and politically ruined.

In spite of all the trouble, Augusta wanted him to win his pending race for the United States Senate.

Life in the Tabor mansion at seventeenth and Broadway just wasn't the same without Horace. Augusta had been sewing quilt blocks all day and was weary. She put away her sewing and stood, looking out of one of the beautiful parlor windows. She was alone in the room and looking toward the west at the mountain range in the distance. Augusta mused, "Yes, up there behind those mountains is Leadville. All the wealth from there has given us everything we could ever want. No need to work hard now. But wait, these are only the material things, and what I want most of all is good health and happiness. Both are gone now, and money can't bring either back to me."

Augusta was very unhappy. Again, she looked toward the mountains. The sunset, in a burst of beauty, lighted up the western sky.

Relatives of Augusta often stayed at the mansion, and, of course, Maxcy was there most of the time. Augusta enjoyed the companionship of her relatives and friends. Life would have been unbearable without them.

Sister Rebecca, aware of Augusta's unhappy mood, entered the room. "Come out into the garden, Augusta, the flowers in back are at their peak of glory," she said.

Augusta did not move from her chair, so another sister, Lucy, settled in a chair beside her. Both sisters were guests in the home and anxious to comfort Augusta. Rebecca put her arms around Augusta and said, "Don't feel defeated, perhaps Horace will come back, and you both can start life anew."

"He has refused to return," replied Augusta in a firm tone of voice. Soon Augusta poured out her heart with events of the past: "Life with Horace was always up and down, but I kept persevering. If only Horace would come to his senses! I hate the gossip that prevails continuously.

118

The newspapers run exaggerated articles that are so embarrassing," continued Augusta.

Maxcy entered the room and added a comment, "The cases dragged through the court are hard to cope with. Father's political career will be ended if conditions do not change."

Since the Tabor divorce was a topic of the day, tongues were wagging with this choice gossip. Augusta did not want a divorce.

Augusta arose from her chair and left for her bedroom, as she could not hide her sorrow. She was broken hearted and miserable without Horace.

Augusta retired early, but could not sleep. Thoughts of past life ran through her mind: "We worked so hard in Kansas, trying to be successful at farming. Poor baby Maxcy was sick with ague and teething. My good health was lost then, suffering from ague. I thought I would die. The hardships of pioneer life were hard to bear. Travel in those days was so exhausting, and many did not survive. It is a wonder any of us lived through it all.

"We went to Colorado in search of gold. We both worked diligently, trying to be successful in mining and our general store. I've worked and sacrificed so much to see Horace advance in mining, business enterprises, and a political career. I was always the devoted wife. Without me to help and encourage him, he never would have reached the peak of success he now enjoys. To think that he now shares it all with another woman is humiliating! How could Horace leave me for that blond hussy? God help me as I long to be by his side as his faithful wife and helpmate. I cannot bear the thought of this woman in my rightful place. She reaps the benefits of my labor and basks in the glory of the Tabor fortune.

"Oh God, is there no justice in this world? Horace and I were happy together, and loved our little baby Maxcy. Horace was so proud to have a son to carry the Tabor name."

"Now, in later life, what will the future be? Money does not always bring true happiness," thought Augusta many, many times. "Horace and I have drifted apart. Riches have brought me desperate marital separation and loneliness. Everything is falling apart for me. This is my darkest hour. I think I shall die of a broken heart."

Chapter Seventeen
The Agonies of Augusta . . . The Divorce

Horace obtained a fraudulent divorce at Durango, Colorado. This scheme did not work as Augusta claimed she had never received a copy of the complaint. This secret Durango divorce was granted April 11, 1882, but was declared illegal.

Horace had employed William Bush to persuade Augusta to agree to a divorce.

Augusta finally sued for separate maintenance and alimony of $50,000 per year. She charged desertion. She had not then filed a suit for divorce. The outcome was that she could not get alimony or maintenance unless there was a divorce.

Augusta estimated Horace Tabor's wealth at nine million, and she stated that his income was about $100,000 per month.

From the <u>Denver</u> <u>Tribune</u>, April 19, 1882.

Suing for Support and Maintenance

Several days ago, Mrs. Augusta L. Tabor, as wife, instituted suit in the District court against Lieutenant Governor Tabor, charging him with desertion, and praying for the recovery of $50,000 a year for support and maintenance. The complaint alleges that the Governor has refused to support Mrs. Tabor.

While the recent contest for the Senatorial appointment was being waged, a threat was made that the suit would be then commenced, but for reasons readily appreciated the action was deferred until after the appointment had been made.

The complaint sets forth in details a number of instances wherein the Governor refused to pay bills of household expenditure and taxes upon the Tabor estate on Broadway, which is occupied by Mrs. Tabor. She avers, also, that she is compelled to receive boarders and rent rooms in the house to support herself. A striking feature of the proceeding is that the suit is practically brought for alimony, without an accompanying request or clause for divorce. It is claimed that the statutes of Colorado do not anticipate or countenance any such action, and that as there is, in consequence, no jurisdiction, the case will be dismissed. An allegation is made that the Governor had repeatedly offered large sums of money to Mrs.Tabor if she would proceed for a divorce.

In the Governor's defense it is stated, that two years ago he gave to Mrs. Tabor $100,000, which she had judiciously invested in real estate in the city. A portion of that amount purchased an interest in the Windsor Hotel, and the return from this investment last year was $14,000.

In the complaint, the Governor's riches are estimated by schedule as amounting to $9,500,000.

Rocky Mountain News, Vol. XXIII, p. 1, April 20, 1882

The Tabor Trouble
Summary of the Complaint in the Case
The Extent of Mr. Tabor's Property Set Forth

The suit for alimony brought by Mrs. Augusta Tabor against Lieut. Gov. H.A.W. Tabor which has been filed as announced in yesterday's News sets forth a large amount of property as owned by the defendant and probably gives a rather definite estimate of Mr. Tabor's wealth. Mrs. Tabor's bill alleges that they were married at Augusta, Maine, on January 31st, 1857, and came to Colorado in 1859. It alleges that they have since resided here, she acting as a true and faithful wife and remaining with him until July, 1880 when he left their home but made occasional visits to her until January, 1881, after which time he discontinued his visits entirely. It further alleges that he has repeatedly offered her a portion of his large fortune if she would get a divorce from him which she steadily refused notwithstanding she had ample cause for so doing. It is alleged that during their married life they have accumulated a large fortune of which the following is an estimate:

Tabor Opera House block, Denver	$800,000
Tabor block, Denver	250,000
Block 3, H.C. Brown's addition, Denver	100,000
Two 2-story brick dwellings, Denver	20,000
Eight lots, block 98, East Denver	100,000
Four lots, block 107, East Denver	50,000
Ninety-seven shares Denver First Ntl Bank Stock	500,000
Bank of Leadville	100,000
The Coliseum theater, Leadville	20,000
Brick Building, Leadville	20,000
Interest in post office building, Leadville	30,000
Gas Stock and Loan to Company, Leadville	100,000
Five houses in Oro	10,000
House in Malta	1,100
Gunnison Hotel	20,000
Stock in Bank of Gunnison	50,000
Telephone Company Stock	15,000

121

Tabor Mill near Leadville	60,000
Matchless Mine	1,000,000
Henriette, Maid of Erin & Waterloo Mines	1,000,000
Chrysolite	50,000
Breece Iron	300,000
Hibernia	100,000
Glass-Pendery	100,000
Oolite and Group	100,000
Interest in Bull Domingo & Robinson	1,000,000
Smuggler, Lead Chief & Denver City	500,000
Summit County Mines	200,000
San Juan County Mines	200,000
New Mexico Mines	50,000
Interest in Fibre Manufacturing Co., Old Mexico	50,000
Interest in Lands on Mortgage Bonds near Chicago	500,000
275 Acres Near Chicago Stock Yards	50,000
320 Acres Old Homestead in Kansas	15,000
Lots in Manhattan, Kansas	100
Coal Lands in South Park	30,000
Railroad Stocks	50,000
Shares in the Denver Steam Heating Company	10,000
Durango Livery and Stage Line	15,000
Government Bonds	200,000
Twenty-three forty-eighths of Tam O'Shanter Mine	1,000,000
Moneys, Loans, Stocks, Notes and Other Securities	200,000
Diamonds and Jewelry	100,000
Stock in Denver, Utah and Pacific Construction Co.	10,000
Total	**$9,076,100**

It is further alleged that there are other properties which the plaintiff cannot describe, but that she is informed and believes his income amounts to $100,000 per month; that he has not contributed toward her support since January, 1881, and that to support herself she has been obliged to rent rooms and take boarders; that her separate estate has been in judiciously invested and is entirely insufficient to maintain her in a "manner and style commensurate with her rank and station in the community:" that the defendant has threatened to sell the house in which she lives and leave her without a home.

For these reasons the plaintiff asks for support during the pendency of the suit and a sum to cover expenses; for the home property, block, in H.C. Brown's addition; for the sum of $50,000 per year in money. Judge Steck is attorney for the plaintiff.

Horace was growing more impatient day by day.

Augusta finally gave in to her husband's wishes and agreed to the divorce in 1883. She was convinced that the gossip of their marital problems would hinder Horace in his political ambitions. She decided not to jeopardize his future in that respect, so she made the sacrifice.

Augusta was crushed, but she said afterward, "There was nothing else I could do."

She charged desertion and non-support. She was given a property settlement of $250,000 consisting of the Broadway mansion and the La Veta apartments worth $250,000 alone. Another figure published lists a settlement of $300,000.

Augusta had worked by Tabor's side for about 25 years and helped him amass this fortune. The settlement does not seem to be a great amount, considering the total amount of the Tabor fortune, and the income he had at the time.

When the hearing ended, Augusta turned to the judge and asked, "What is my name?"

"Your name is Tabor ma'am. Keep the name. It is yours by rights."

" I will. It is mine till I die, Judge. I ought to thank you for what you have done, but I cannot. I am not thankful, but it was the only thing left for me to do. But, Judge, I wish you would put into the record: not willingly asked for." Augusta walked out of the court in tears, repeating, "Oh God! Not willingly, not willingly!"

Augusta felt deeply wronged by Tabor. She cherished the hope that he would some day return to her. She felt that sometime Tabor would need money. She knew his ways very well and felt his fortune would be eventually gone. No doubt Baby Doe would desert him then. Surely she would not want an old man --- only his money. In 1893, when the money was gone, Augusta offered to help him. He refused; his pride restrained him.

Denver society rallied to Augusta's support after the divorce. Maxcy also stood by his mother Augusta, much to the disappointment and anger of Horace.

Augusta revealed her feelings concerning Baby Doe to a reporter from the Denver Republican, which read as follows: "She is a blonde, I understand, and paints. Mr. Tabor has changed a great deal. He used to detest women of that kind. He would never allow me to whitewash my face, however much I desired to. She wants his money and will hang on to him as long as he has got a nickel. She don't want an old man."

The reporter ventured to suggest that Mr. Tabor was not such an old man. "Oh yes he is! He dyes his hair and mustache. I noticed him in the courtroom the other day. He was afraid to draw his handkerchief across his mouth for fear of staining it."

On October 31,1883, the Denver Post carried an article by a reporter that interviewed Augusta which ran as follows: "I told you when you came in that I had been reading about Senator Tabor. I preserve everything I see about him. I have three scrapbooks full."

Augusta reminisced about former days and again related the account of the Hook and Rische discovery as follows: I was coming downstairs, and Rische rushed into the room with his hands full of specimens shouting "We've struck it!"

I said to him rather frigidly, "I expect Rische, when you bring me the money instead of rocks, I'll believe you." Her indifference is not to be wondered, considering the many years of first hope and then disappointment that Augusta had experienced.

Augusta Tabor's letter to husband Horace Tabor, September 3, 1881, Denver, where she implores him to take her to the opening at the Tabor Grand Opera House:

> *I am in town and would like very much to go to the Tabor Grand and witness the glory that you are to receive. Believe me, that none will be more proud of it than your broken hearted wife. Will you not take me there and by so doing, stop the gossip that is busy with our affairs. God knows that I am truly sorry for our estrangement and will humble myself in the dust at your feet if you will only return. Whatever I said to you was done in the heat of passion, and you know the awful condition that I was in when it was said . . . Pity, I beseech you, and forgive me...and let us bury the past and commence anew, and my life shall be devoted to you forever. Your loving wife,"*

Horace did not respond to Augusta's plea for his return and their reconciliation.

A letter from Augusta Tabor to Horace Tabor, Jan. 31, 1883, Denver.

> *Dear Husband,*
>
> *I am happy to say that I am not divorced, and that you are still mine. All the intimidations and threats were of no avail. When I went into court and swore that I had not consented to it willingly and I have since ascertained that the divorce is null and void. Now this is the 26th anniversary of our wedding. Just such a storm as we are having today we were married in, and surely we did not live in a storm all those 24 years that you were at home. Now you have had the honors of Senateship, which you deserted me for. And when your month is out, come home and let us live in harmony, or I will come to you. There is no need of having our case dragged through court again. And as I am your wife, I shall stand upon my rights. I have consulted several prominent judges and they all tell me that it was a farce. Even Judge Steck will not tell me that it will stand. Therefore, I subscribe myself your loving wife.*
>
> *Mrs. H.A.W. Tabor*

Chapter Eighteen
The Senate Race and H.A.W. Tabor's Speech

Governor Tabor was a Republican, and almost singly supported the Republican party. He donated about $200,000. Two U.S. Senators were to be elected. Tabor did not win the full term. His opponent, Judge Bowen, was elected by a majority of one vote. Tabor only got the 30-day term to fill the vacancy left by Henry Teller. (Teller had been appointed Secretary of the Interior.)

Mr. Tabor's speech:

Mr. President and brethren of the Pioneer Association of Colorado: In response to the sentiment just offered, you will not expect from an humble hard-working pioneer like myself any exhibition of eloquence or fancy, or poetry, for you all know that I am no orator as a Brutus, but a plain blunt-spoken man. Born amidst the green mountains of Vermont about a half century ago, and having passed my early life amidst the pure breezes of liberty, where the clank of the slaves shackle was never heard, and having achieved independence of character, action and thought, with the tools of my trade as a stonecutter. I early turned my eyes toward the great West. Seeing in my mind's eye the tide of population as it swept onward, from the stormy Atlantic to the tranquil sea, I folded my tent and worked my way from the valleys and mountains of New England to the plains of Kansas. And there at Topeka, as a member of its first legislature, the iron entered my soul, as we were forcibly dispersed, like the chamber of deputies in Paris, by the despotic orders of the then president; and my attachment to the union and its constitution and flag became deeper and deeper from its attempt to extend slavery into the territories then free; for I was an humble soldier in the ranks of the grand old Whig party, led on by Clay and Webster whose watchword was contained in the grand declaration "non-interference with slavery where the constitution protects it, and non-extension of it into the territories where it did not exist." But soon after these stirring events, I caught the fever

125

of excitement, as the news came back from west to east that the base of Pikes Peak rested upon fields of gold; and so in 1859, with the other pioneers, many of whom are now present, I plodded my weary way to Colorado and shovel in hand, as a gold seeker, by hard manual labor, I earned my first wages at the beautiful town of Idaho Springs. The reminiscences and associations conjured up by looking back over this period of my early life overwhelm me, and my tongue becomes silent at the thoughts of our country at that time, of my own humble situation, and of the changes and chances that have overtaken our union and myself since then and have given us this beautiful city, these fertile valleys, fat with corn, these mountains and these hills covered with ten-thousand flocks. This land of ours, literally flowing with milk and honey, instead of those dusty plains, those sterile prairies that then made it the Great American Desert. Since that period our southern boundary has been extended to the Gulf of Mexico; and our western clear over to the Pacific.

And after a fratricidal war, unequaled in the number of its troops, the skill, courage and power of both its armies, today thank God the sun shines on that dear old flag, and the prophecy fulfilled; for henceforth united we stand and forever and forever shall have but one constitution, one country, one destiny. Nay, more, our whole Union is bound in bonds of iron, and three great international highways are transporting from sea to sea its rich products, and the representatives from the Parliaments of Great Britain and of Europe, and the millionaires of all the world, are astonished and amazed at this empire of free men, who manage and control a government for free men only, but I must stop.

Passing on from Idaho Springs to California gulch, in Lake County, and enduring all the privations and sufferings of a pioneer, living for years in my humble log cabin, whose latch-string was always on the outside, and watching and waiting for the good times, I was certain would come; finally, by pluck, patience and perseverance and with the aid of my hard-working companions and friends, we "struck it rich," and fortune smiled upon my labors and spread out around my feet the Leadville carbonates in boundless profusion giving me a larger amount than others. Having been reared in the schools of adversity, I hope and trust I was neither carried away nor rendered foolish nor giddy by the triumphant success that has crowned my labors for so many years, and so thanking God for His kindness to me and mine, I sought to use His good gifts for the benefits of my old companions and brother pioneers and friends. Looking to the great needs of the city of

126

Leadville I endeavored, without pride or vanity to contribute to its comforts and its wants in education, religion, journalism, commerce, currency, and taste; and fast as I possessed the means, I used them there; not to build lordly palaces, not to invest in government bonds, nor to give tawdry and vulgar entertainments, nor to ride through our own land and Europe in princely palace cars, but for the erection of newspapers, schools, churches, gas works, banking houses, theaters, city halls, engine houses and fire engines, and today I can point with pride to my old home in Leadville as the most productive, substantial, and rich, comfortable home of miners on this earth. Its mineral product this year will amount to $18,000,000. And within the boundaries of its mountain streets every human wish and want can be gratified. But as we dug and delved, and burrowed in the mountains of Leadville, the God of fortune, and Fortune herself, still smiled on all my efforts and crowned with success all my labors, and in the rich carbonates of the Matchless, Dunkin, Chrysolite, Denver City, Henrietta and others, I found ample means to proceed in the great works of improvements that had grown in my fancy and purposes, since my first fortunate strike. Coming to Denver, the loveliest village of the plain, I foresaw without the gift of prophecy that it must soon become the political capital of Colorado, and that in the long future, with its temples dedicated to God, to learning, to science, to talent, to art, to hospitality and refinement, it must grow to be the Athens of the great West and so I went to work to contribute my share, now while I had the means to lay its foundations broad and deep, and to erect here, at the foot of those gorgeous mountains, monument more enduring than brass or iron.

The only benefit that I sought to derive from these expenditures was that in common with all our people I could contribute to the comfort, the enjoyment and refinement of the present; and also to secure homes, schools, churches, palaces, dedicated to pointing, to the drama, to the repose and absolute enjoyment of the home life of the stranger within our gates. And there they stand; and there they will remain, long years from now, when Denver shall become the great metropolis of the mountains, monuments of the humble source from whence they came.

Pardon me; I speak this in no language of vanity; for, had I been governed by that alone, I might have expended my resources in family dwellings costing millions; in fancy horses, using hundreds of thousands; in magnificent yachts, exhausting millions, and drowning in their reckless expeditions the humble pilot boat that could not escape their wicked and cruel speed. But to me there is greater pleasure in listening with the crowd to the magnificent representations of Barrett and Mc Cullough of their wondrous performances of "Francesea de Rimini," and Virginlus " and hearing the plaudits of the weary traveler as he emerges from the Windsor; and the acclamations of joy that are heard in the art gallery of the opera house, than even in the pecuniary income derived from my investment and from my very heart of hearts, I thank my God, and my fortune too, that I have been enabled to first become a pioneer of Colorado, and secondly to have contributed in my humble way so much to its early beginning and its future welfare and in the future, as in the past, should fortune still continue to smile upon me, I propose to follow the same line of duty; and permit no man to excel me in my contributions to the public good of my adopted state.

Having already passed two thirds of the milestones that lead to the grave, and having witnessed the evidence of all popular applause, and the bitter ingratitude that follows in the wake of favors bestowed on individuals . . . the utter uncertainty and instability of popular favor . . . I look forward to the time when I shall sleep in my own home in yonder beautiful Riverside. And when I have laid me down to rest besides the Iliffs, Whittsitts and others of our old pioneer brotherhood, I trust that then, if not till then, justice will be done to my motives and my memory, and that in truth and charity there will be engraved on my tombstone . . .

H.A.W. Tabor Mansion at 13th and Sherman Streets, Denver, Colorado. Photo courtesy of the Denver Public Library Western Collection.

A painting of Baby Doe Tabor, second wife of H.A.W. Tabor, shown by her wedding gown. The wedding outfit cost $7,000. Photo courtesy of the Library of the State Historical Society of Colorado Collection.

Elizabeth Bonduel Lily Tabor, first daughter of Horace and Baby Doe Tabor. Photo courtesy of the Library of the State Historical Society of Colorado Connection.

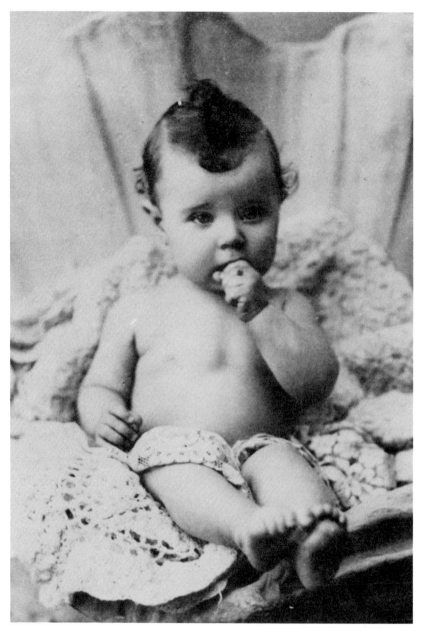

Rosemary Echo Silver Dollar Tabor, second daughter of Horace and Baby Doe Tabor. Photo courtesy of the Library of the State Historical Society of Colorado Collection.

Chapter Nineteen
Another Marriage

While H.A.W. Tabor was United States Senator, he and Baby Doe were married March 1, 1883 in Washington, D.C. This elaborate and fashionable wedding took place at the Willard Hotel. President Chester Arthur and his cabinet were in attendance. The women invited refused to attend, and no women were in attendance except for the relatives of Baby Doe.

The bride wore a wedding outfit costing $7,000. Father Chapelle performed the ceremony. The following day he learned that both Horace Tabor and his bride had been previously married and divorced. Incensed at what he considered a deception, he returned the $200 fee. Nothing concerning the wedding appears in church records. Denver newspapers broke the story that Horace and Baby Doe had been secretly married Sept. 30, 1882, in St. Louis. This was three months before his divorce from Augusta was final. Along with the Durango, Colorado, divorce granted April 11, 1882, this scandal was subject to much gossip.

Horace and Baby Doe returned to Denver where they lived extravagantly for about 10 years.

After the wedding, the Tabors made their home in the Windsor Hotel in Denver. They remained in this beautiful suite until moving to the mansion at 13th and Sherman streets.

From the Denver Tribune, March 11, 1883: "Tabor's Wedding-Colonel W. H. Bush Very Indignant About the Malicious Vaporings of the Press."

From the Kansas City Journal:

The register of the Union depot hotel yesterday attracted the attention of a "Journal" wanderer, for there at the bottom of the page was inscribed in modest and retiring characters, the name of William H. Bush, Denver, Colorado, a man well known as the most intimate friend and advisor of Senator Tabor, who has for some time past occupied a goodly portion of newspaper space, owing to his peculiar much married condition. Sending up his card the reporter received an invitation to come up to Mr. Bush's room. Entering, he was cordially received and after some desultory remarks the reporter remarked that it was generally understood that Mr. Bush was Senator Tabor's closest friend and knew most of him and referred to the recent wedding, and the talk which it was giving rise to. In answer to a question as to whether he would tell what he knew of the subject Mr. Bush replied: "Very willingly, sir." "Well, then said the reporter, "first of all is there any truth in the St. Louis Republican's story of the previous marriage in St. Louis?" "There is not one grain of truth in the statement. It is lie from beginning to end." But Mr. Bush at this juncture seemed rather warm about the collar. "But, Mr. Bush," continued the scribe, "they seem to give all the details very accurately, also the names." "I don't care for that. I repeat it with emphasis, there is not a word of truth in it. The newspapers in this country have misrepresented the old man in every possible way. They have lied first about one thing and then about another until it seems that they are unable to tell the truth where he is concerned. They have been trying to make it appear that he is a vulgar, illiterate, shoddy Senator, when the truth is, that a quieter, more unassuming man does not live. One of the papers in Washington had it that he paid $250 for each of the night shirts in his wedding outfit. Now I don't believe that Tabor ever had a night shirt that cost over $5. That is a little thing but it is a fair sample of how he has been lied about."

"Who is this Miss Mc Court?" asked the reporter.

"She is, or rather was, the divorced wife of Harvey Doe, a miner and prospector. I first knew them about four years ago when I kept the Teller House at Central City, Colorado. He was then working in a mine called the Fourth of July, and made a failure of it. His wife at that time was as devoted to him as a woman could be. When he failed, they went down to Black Hawk, and thence drifted to Denver, where she left him because he would not, or could not, support her. She then went to Oshkosh, Wisconsin, to live with her mother, and has since divided her time between Oshkosh, New York and Chicago. In each of the last two cities she has a sister living."

"Where did Senator Tabor first meet her?"

"In New York last summer she visited Denver and remained for a short time, and then went back to the East. I think that the marriage was arranged then. That visit of hers gave rise to the pretty story the papers are telling about Senator Tabor fitting up a magnificent suite of rooms for her at the Windsor in Denver. I know that no such thing was done."

"How about the reports concerning his divorce from his first wife?"

"That is another one of the newspaper lies. Tabor told me two years ago that he and his wife were living very unhappily together, and asked me about procuring a divorce . . . what I thought of it, etc. I strongly opposed the scheme, and told him that it would give his enemies a chance to talk about him; but he finally convinced me that it was the best thing to do. I do not wish to say what influenced me in changing my opinions, but I had good ones, only I shall not publish them to the world."

"Is there any foundation for the sensational reports?"

"Nothing, sir, whatever. It is a shame that people will talk in this manner of a thing that they know nothing of. I blame the newspapers for it all."

"What has become of Doe?"

"Oh, he is living with his father, I believe, at Idaho Springs. He does not amount to much, and never did. And now I must say good morning. I hope you will do better than most of the newspapers have done, and tell the truth about Tabor."

From The <u>Denver</u> <u>Tribune</u>, April 19, 1883.

A Tribute To Tabor - The Ex-Senator and His Wife
Handsomely Serenaded by the German Societies

A large number of citizens forming the Maennerchof and Turner Laederstaffer societies, representing the German element of the city, manifested their appreciation and bestowed a handsome compliment upon Senator Tabor and his wife at the Windsor hotel last evening. The German citizens of Denver regard Senator Tabor with a sentiment of gratitude for the many personal and business benefits which he has bestowed by his industry, his perseverance and great-heartedness in public enterprise.

The members of these societies, numbering about one hundred persons, assembled in the hall in front of Mr. Tabor's suite of rooms, about half past 9 o'clock last evening, and tendered the distinguished couple a delightful serenade, each society alternating the songs. After the serenade the party was invited into the rooms and hospitably entertained by Governor Tabor and wife, who were assisted by Mrs. and Miss Wurtzenbach, Colonel Wurtzebach and Mr. Mc Court. Quartets were sung, also solos, toasts were drank, and speeches made by Messrs. Adolph Reichere, Wurtzebach, Rieck, Whist, Leimer, Adams and Herman Leuders.

In the midst of the pleasant entertainment, a beautiful floral offering, the gift of Mr. Charles F. Miller, was presented to Mrs.

Tabor by Mr. A. Schuneman, who made the following neat little speech:

Senator Tabor and Lady:

We come here to welcome you home again as a member of our society, an organization whose objects consists of educating our youth, not only in physical but in moral development. You have been one of the first Americans to identify yourself with our organization, which is the more praiseworthy because as an American we scarcely had a right to expect it of you.

Permit me in conclusion to express the thanks of our society for the honor which has been conferred upon you by your election as United States Senator, which honor you appreciated and are worthy of.

But most of all we assembled here to honor to you as a fellow citizen, the most enterprising in Colorado, whose aim has ever been, to improve not only our city, but the entire state. Once more, Mr. Senator, welcome home.

When the pleasant greetings were over at the Windsor, Mr. Tabor was escorted by the societies to the East Turner Hall, where the tables were spread with refreshments and wine, and here an hour was passed with music and good cheer, including many happy toasts to the honored guest.

There was a pause in the merrymaking when Mr. Tabor was called upon for a speech. He modestly thanked the society for their compliment to himself and wife, and assured them that the latch string of his house was always on the outside to them.

Mr. Schunenam was called upon for a speech, and he related many incidents in the life of Mr. Tabor wherein he proved himself a friend to the people, both in his poor pioneer life and in his rich estate. He characterized Mr. Tabor as the father of Leadville and Denver, and heartily endorsed him as the next Governor of Colorado.

Then followed other speeches and songs, and near midnight the company dispersed in happy spirits.

Two daughters were born to the Tabors. The first was Elizabeth Bonduel Lily, born July 13, 1884, and Rose Mary Echo Silver Dollar, born December 17, 1889. A son was born October 17, 1888, but died on the same date.

Now living in Denver, Horace and Baby Doe made unsuccessful attempts to enter society. Baby Doe was snubbed by the elite. Society refused to accept her. Damaging rumors were circulated concerning the Tabors, hinting that financial reverses were overtaking the millionaire.

Soon it was a reality that the last remnants of a million-dollar fortune were slipping through the hands of H.A.W. Tabor. The ex-Senator was forced to give up property after property --- sold under the hammer.

During the silver panic of 1893, H.A.W. Tabor lost everything. It brought him and his second family virtual pauperism. Much of the Tabor fortune was also lost through unfortunate investments, mostly in other states. He lost huge sums in South America and Mexico.

To the surprise of many, the second Mrs. Tabor did not pack her trunks and leave after the Tabor fortune was lost. She sold her gorgeous diamonds and parted with her expensive wardrobe in a last effort to get cash.

The Tabors lost the beautiful mansion at 13th and Sherman streets. They moved into the Tabor Opera House block to live. Eventually they were living in cheaper rented houses.

Tabor did not despair. He said, "I will rise to where I was and even higher." Again, Horace persevered.

Chapter Twenty
Where Is The Luck?

Recollections of the Tabor Family By Z. Fuller, MD.:

During my residence in Denver from 1884 to 1894 I saw and heard much of the Tabors, then much in the public eye. The Tabor Grand Opera House, conceded to be the finest thing of the kind west of the Mississippi, and the pride of Denver and Colorado, had recently been built. Senator Tabor had his headquarters in the Opera Block, where I also had an office, and later had offices nearby in Curtis and Arapahoee Streets, so I saw the Senator often, who was actively about the Block and the near-by streets.

The Senator was then about fifty years old, although he appeared older than that. Rather "stock", medium height and weight, a bit stooped, with gait of long stride like a countryman; dark-skinned, rugged, strong face, clean-shaven except a heavy, dark, drooping mustache; on the whole, something of the look of a foreigner, perhaps Jewish. Dressed always in black, a prince Albert coat, silk hat, he was a rather striking figure. When about, he met many people to whom he bowed or greeted otherwise, some with a hand-shake and perhaps a brief moment of conversation but rarely more, seemingly having few if any intimate friends, being in bad odor in the community because of his domestic antics; the first Mrs. Tabor having all but universal sympathy. So there was an air of sadness about the Senator. I never saw him smile. Clearly his wealth had not brought him happiness or contentment.

The Truth About Tabor as printed in The Colorado Graphic, Vol. 4, No. 1, p.1, col. 6, Sept. 1, 1888

"He has been vilified more than any man ever was before in politics. The sleuth hounds of those who refused to serve have followed him into his private business, to try to wreck his fortune. The sanctity of his family life has been invaded and made a subject of public criticism and attempted ridicule. The leaders of the party

137

in the state have slapped him on both cheeks and spat in his face. He has never wavered in his allegiance to his party, the state, to the people, nor to his manhood. His contributions have always been liberal and his work has always been hard for party victory.

"In 1884 when he was a candidate for governor, he was needlessly assailed in two or three public speeches made by a prominent leader of the party whose own moral residence was constructed entirely of very frail glass. He felt these assaults keenly. He was shamefully treated in the state convention, and if ever men had cause from the heaping on insult on injury and perfidy on injustice to desert a party, he certainly had in the campaign of that year. Far from such a course was his policy. No sooner had the convention adjourned than he set himself to work to bring about a compromise in Arapahoe County, which he effected and then he gave freely of his money and his time to elect the ticket. Before he would accept the chairmanship of the state commission in 1886 he received the personal pledge of all the prominent party men of the state that they would help him in the campaign. Unfortunately, those pledges were not kept, and, except, from ex-Senator Hill, he received but very little aid from the party leaders. He bore the burden of the campaign himself, without complaint and worked day and night for the success of the ticket. Two-thirds of the campaign expenses he paid out of his own pocket.

"It is perhaps useless to comment on the result of the campaign of 1886, but such confidence, respect and affection have the rank and file of the party in the state for ex-Senator Tabor, that it is safe to say that had he not been chairman of the committee a good portion of the balance of the ticket would have been defeated. An incident occurred in the campaign which illustrated the unselfishness of the man and his devotion to duty and to party. One of the candidates on the ticket was an editor. In 1884 when Tabor was a candidate for the nomination for governor the candidate referred to had bitterly denounced him and attacked his family affairs and reflected quite severely on his wife. Tabor had never seen these articles. Naturally such assaults read for the first time, would arouse a spirit of revenge in most any man. Tabor read the articles, put the papers away and said not a word to any one about them until after the campaign was over. The candidate referred to did not pay his assessment, but Tabor made up the amount himself and paid the expense of holding meetings for said candidate at the principal towns in the state. Of course this candidate is still of the opinion that Mr. Tabor is not fit for any position and that he (the candidate) is a very great man.

"The time has come in Colorado politics, we hope, when such men as ex-Senator Tabor will be treated as they deserve. There is no position in the gift of the party which he has not earned, and to which, by all rules of right and justice, he is not fairly entitled. The repeated attacks on Tabor led a great many people to believe that he is not adapted to public life. Few men in the state are better adapted to it. He has splendid executive ability, an abundance of tact, is well posted on matters of public importance, has clear, keen perceptions and an inexhaustible fund of good humor. He is an entertaining companion, a true friend and a sincere man. He impresses every person with his frankness, and has great control over those with whom he comes in contact."

Horace Tabor continued to be occupied with business and politics.

In 1891 he was chosen president of the Denver Chamber of Commerce and Board of Trade.

Winfield Scott Stratton, a Cripple Creek millionaire, gave Tabor $15,000 as a loan. This was encouraging, and Horace made preparations to start mining again.

I have a copy of an original old newspaper that states the money Tabor received from Stratton was $10,000 and given in ten-one thousand dollar bills. Stratton did not expect it to be repaid as a loan unless Tabor struck ore and had the means to repay it. (Years ago Senator Tabor advanced some money to Winfield S. Stratton when he was a poor struggling miner. Stratton never had forgotten it.) Now he came to the aid of Tabor.

Horace Tabor went to Cripple Creek and Boulder County. This area was rich in gold. The move to Ward was made in 1897, where he developed the Eclipse Mine. While in Ward, he staked out a claim and built a cabin. As a start, he furnished the cabin with about $50 worth of furniture. This and a few mining tools comprised all his worldly possessions. His wife (Baby Doe) and two daughters accompanied him. Horace worked diligently trying to strike pay dirt once more. These mining ventures failed because of lack of capital, consequently, Tabor ran out of funds. He wanted to continue his work, and it was a great disappointment to have to leave what he had done before striking ore. If only he could have had more funds to continue, he felt he might have been successful.

President William Mc Kinley appointed H.A.W. Tabor postmaster of Denver in 1898. It was through the influence of Senator Walcott that this appointment came to Horace Tabor. Mr. Tabor deserved this honor, having played an important political and economic role in the development of Denver and Colorado. (Previously he had donated the ground to the city for this post office.)

Now, with a regular income, Horace and his family lived again in the Windsor Hotel. This time they occupied less expensive and smaller quarters.

Illustrated Sentinel, Vol. 8, No. 30, April 20, 1898, Denver, Colorado.

H.A.W. Tabor-Weighing The Mail

The revenue of the Denver post office has increased very materially the past year, and the work of the present force of employees has increased accordingly. Highlands, with its ten thousand inhabitants and four square miles of territory, was added to the free delivery system last fall and the department appointed only three carriers to do the vast amount of work there. When the Hon. H.A.W. Tabor took charge of the Denver post office last February he was not long in seeing that extra help was needed, and must be had, to do justice to the public and relieve the overworked clerks and carriers of the Denver Post office. Mr. Tabor has taken hold of the work of the office with an energy that means progress, and he consults daily with the heads of the departments to get well posted with the workings and find out the needs of the office. Mr. I.P. Kelley, superintendent of city delivery, who has been an employee of the Denver post office for nearly fifteen years, and knows better the amount of work being done and the pressing needs of the office at the present time than any other man, has assisted Mr. Tabor very much with his work.

Mr. Tabor decided to prepare an itemized statement of each carriers work to send to the department at Washington. He has had each of the seventy-six letter carriers of the Denver post office make out a written statement of the work he does daily. This statement records number of trips made each day, number of blocks walked each day while on duty, number of stairways to be climbed, number of buildings with elevators in, etc. The Bundy time clocks that each carrier must ring up every time he enters or leaves the office, record the exact amount of time used each day, and no regular carrier is allowed to work more than eight hours any day. In addition to this Mr. Tabor has had superintendent Kelley weigh each carriers mail as he left the office for ten days, and it is the results of the weighing that show most clearly the vast amount of work being done and the awful loads that are being taken out by the carriers of the Denver post office. Superintendent Kelley weighed each carriers mail separately on each trip for the ten days, and Postmaster Tabor will submit this itemized statement of weights along with the size of each carriers route and the time used, to the department at Washington. Number of carriers delivering mail, 76; collecting, 3; total area delivered, about 32 square miles; number of deliveries in business district, between fourteenth and nineteenth streets and between Union depot and state capitol, 5 trips daily; residence districts, 2 trips each day; total amount of mail delivered in the ten days, 47,821 pounds, almost twenty-four tons; first class mail, letters delivered, 5,028 pounds; second class mail, letters and packages delivered, 42,793 pounds; average amount of mail delivered daily by each one of the seventy-six carriers, 62.92 pounds; daily average of first class mail, 13.23 pounds; daily average of second class mail, 49.69 pounds. The number of letters to the pound averages 55, making an average of 728 letters delivered daily by each carrier. Route 41, at the Equitable building and Albany hotel, had the highest average. In the ten days, the carrier delivered 1,440 pounds of mail, and average of 144 pounds each day; his first class mail averaged 48.90 pounds per day; the heaviest letter mail he carried out on one trip was 30 pounds, or 1,650 letters; the last five days his route was taken by a substitute, and he has had to work over twelve hours each day to dispose of the vast amount of mail. Carriers 62, 55 and 63 take out almost as much mail as is carried out on route 41. The heaviest mail taken out on one trip was carried on route 16, a residence district just north of the state capitol; 84 pounds was the load. The carrier would have to work perhaps three hours to dispose of that mail, and at the same time collect the mail from the street boxes as he came to them, and accept all the letters and Sunday papers the ladies of the route have ready for him as he comes along, so that when he has finished his delivery and returned to the office his load has diminished only about one-half, and he must go over the same route in the afternoon.

Right here let us remark that the present system of collecting mail at the Denver post office is one of the greatest detriments to the progress of the service. With only three collectors, they can only collect mail in the business districts and not as often there as it should be done. In the residence districts if a letter is dropped in the street box just after the carrier has passed on his afternoon delivery, say at 3:30 o'clock, it is not taken out and mailed at the office until noon the next day. With the perfect street car system of Denver, the best of any city of its size in the United States, the Denver post office should have a system of street car collections

141

that will deliver mail at the office from any part of the city within one hour from the time it is dropped in the box. By weighing the mail it is found that the carriers in the business district making five trips each day take out the most mail, while the carriers of the residence districts making two trips each day carry less mail, but their loads are heavier, they walk further and they are obliged to collect all mail from their routes. In addition to this all carriers of the office must take out registered mail on their routes and get a receipt for each piece from the person to whom it is directed; he must keep a record of all letters addressed on his route that he cannot deliver; he must record all removal orders, and forward the mail as directed elsewhere in the city or out of the city, as the case may be, In fact, he must be the postmaster of the district where he delivers mail.

Mr. Tabor has shown excellent business judgment in having this itemized report prepared, and when it is forwarded to Washington we feel sure that it will so clearly define the work, the progress and the needs of the Denver post office that the department will immediately issue orders for the necessary number of clerks and carriers, so that the work of the Denver office may be done the best of any office in the United States.

S.R. Purdy

Chapter Twenty-one
The Truth About Augusta Tabor
and
The Declining Years

Histories of the Tabors have often contained unfair and incorrect descriptions of Augusta Tabor, such as: "She was a straight-laced New Englander, cold and flat chested, and not very pretty." Others have been of the opinion that Augusta dressed in somber colors and was not interested in fancy dress or jewelry.

In reality, she was a warm, loving, and kind person. The following is a paragraph stating the opinions of one of Augusta's many friends that knew her as far back as the early days of prospecting:

An old miner friend of Augusta's expressed his admiration of her and said, "I knew Mrs. Tabor for years in California Gulch. There was never a harder working woman nor a bigger-hearted one. If she had but one meal between her and starvation, she would share it with anyone in want. We "Old Timers" saw some rough days together and had a chance to find out what sort of stuff each was made of, and I will say it: "Horace Tabor had a mighty good wife; one that stuck by him through thick and thin--in the years he was struggling, and he ought not to forget it."

During the prosperity of the Tabors, there was much entertainment held at the Tabor mansion. An account of these affairs always appeared in the newspapers. Along with the guest list, appeared a description of the gowns and jewelry worn by the ladies.

I have a description of a reception that took place during the heyday of the Tabors. Contained in this article is another instance of Augusta's manner of dress. Especially memorable were the receptions held on New Years. A description of Augusta's attire is as follows: Mrs. Tabor wore an exquisite blue moiré and satin, heavily hand embroidered. She wore a new set of costly diamonds which were highly admired by all the guests.

Over 200 leading gentlemen of the city were in attendance and went away expressing their delight with the entire affair. These men were prominent in commerce, politics, law, medicine and journalism. Most were dressed in swallow-tails and white kids. Those who came in

143

business suits were not slighted. The ladies gave them the most attention in order to make them feel welcome. The spacious parlors of the Tabor mansion were the best facilities in the entire city for this sort of a reception . Gas lights burned brightly. Dancing took place at intervals to the music of the piano. To the delight of all, Mrs. Leet, a Louisiana, French lady, upon request, sang some selections from the French Opera.

The great social accomplishments of Miss Fisher and Miss Needles, and other ladies, helped in making the affair a pleasant one. Miss Lou Babcock, the prettiest young lady in Denver, was by Augusta's side, always assisting her in any way possible.

Refreshments consisted of every delicacy obtainable. No liquors were offered. Mrs. Tabor felt that liquor should be banished from New Year's receptions. (She had served nothing stronger than coffee the previous year.) She felt that stimulants at a reception were not needed in order to have a delightful time. She was justly proud of the calls she received and warm expressions of esteem given by the guests.

Contrary to the opinion that Augusta did not want or wear beautiful clothes, we find descriptions that her wardrobe consisted of many beautiful gowns and clothes of the latest fashion. Augusta always dressed with good taste and owned beautiful and costly jewelry.

During my research, I met a person back East and discovered, in an interview with her, that she knew of a fine piece of Mrs. Tabor's jewelry that had been handed down to a relative of Augusta's. Augusta had purchased this certain piece in Italy and was known to collect precious items such as this on her travels abroad.

"What sort of person was Augusta?" ask many on tour of the Tabor Opera House. Often she has not been given credit for her outstanding and good qualities of character. Once again, I try to set the records straight with the truth about Augusta. Her character was of the best and beyond reproach. She had a good upbringing and received a good education in Maine.

At the beginning of this book, I have given credit to Augusta as being a beautiful young lady. Her newly discovered photographs are testimony to that fact.

Not only was Augusta Tabor one of the best known women in Colorado, but she was also one of the wealthiest.

During the prosperity of Denver, her wealth was estimated at $3,000,000, consisting chiefly of real estate in the best part of Denver.

The divorce settlement of 1883 was between $250,000 and $300,000. She had invested it wisely and built up her estate to the $3,000,000 figure. Augusta had increased all her wealth by her remarkable ability and good judgment in business. She was shrewd in choosing her investments, and they all brought good returns. She used careful management in all her vast holding.

In Denver, Augusta Tabor continued her membership in the Unity Church and was also one of the most active members of the Pioneer Ladies' Aid Society. (She was said to have had broad religious views.)

She gave much to charity, always helping the poor and less fortunate. She responded generously to any request for aid.

She often had lawn parties and socials for the benefit of the Unity Church. The decorations were elaborate and fitting for the occasion or season of the year. For the lawn parties, there was always brilliant illumination, the latest of the time. Fine music added to the entertainments. Everyone in attendance always reported having a wonderful time.

Augusta's lawn, surrounding the mansion, was huge. It was all beautifully designed with flower gardens, shrubs and trees. The beauty of it all formed a pleasing landscape. The entire grounds gave an overall view of a small park. People passing by the Tabor property looked at and admired this wonderful addition to Denver's choice downtown area.

The Declining Years: As we have previously learned, Augusta Tabor, before the divorce, was closely associated with H.A.W. Tabor. They led a very adventurous and exciting style of life. Together, in the early days of the development of Colorado, they played a great part in the building of the state.

After the divorce, Augusta's life was completely changed. She continued living in the Broadway mansion for years, but lived quietly. She seemed to only want the companionship of her relatives and close friends. She found a restful evening at home comforting. She did not care to take part in public or social life of Denver. Thus, Augusta was somewhat withdrawn from the activities of her previous life.

Eventually, she gave up the mansion, leased the building to the Commercial Club and continued to live quietly at the Brown Palace Hotel. Later, she lived at a residence on Lincoln Avenue between 16th and 17th streets.

Augusta had been in poor health for several years. Under her doctor's excellent care, she still seemed to be ailing and had not shown signs of improvement. She suffered with lung afflictions and a nervous numbness of the nature of paralysis. Therefore, her physician strongly advised her to go to a lower altitude. Maxcy and other relatives were concerned about her condition and encouraged Augusta to do everything possible to restore her health.

At first thought, Augusta was reluctant to move away from those so dear to her. After careful consideration, she decided in favor of a move to California. (Augusta remained in Denver until the middle of November, as she wanted to vote before going to California.)

By November of 1894, she was comfortably settled in the Balmoral Hotel in Pasadena, California. (Pasadena still holds the reputation of being a winter resort for the rich and the famous. However, so many of these old, wonderful hotels have been torn down today. It is encouraging to learn that demolition of these great old landmarks has been stopped and many have been restored.)

Augusta soon adjusted to the new environment in a sunny and warm climate. She relaxed in the comforts of this fine hotel which offered all desirable facilities. Relatives and friends were happy to learn that Augusta was now showing improvement.

Maxcy, in Denver, was relieved with the good news that his mother's health was improving and that she was steadily gaining strength. He could now settle down to his regular routine at the Brown Palace Hotel.

Suddenly, a telegram arrived informing him that his mother's health had worsened, and that she had become dangerously ill. Maxcy rushed to his mother's bedside, but she died on January 30, 1895, just before his arrival.

Poor Maxcy was overwhelmed with grief and in a state of terrible shock. Along with other complications, chronic bronchitis and pneumonia were listed as the immediate cause of her death.

Chapter Twenty-two
The Death of Augusta Tabor

<u>The place</u>: The Balmoral Hotel, Pasadena, California
<u>The time</u>: January 30, 1895

Augusta, in her living quarters, paced the floor nervously. She was concerned about her ailments. Now, to add to her misery, she had a very bad cold. Her doctor had just diagnosed it as bronchitis and pneumonia. This terrible cold had confined Augusta to her bed the past few days, and now conditions had worsened. Having difficulty breathing, she arose from her bed and walked the floor. She felt very weak and distressed. "I hope I do not faint," thought Augusta. "I am so cold, and I must go back to bed."

Lying there alone, she was aware of noises around the hotel. People were coming and going down the hallways and stairways.

Alone with her thoughts and memories of the past, visions raced through her mind. . . she thought of herself as a young girl, living happily in Maine, meeting Horace, the courtship, the marriage, homesteading in Kansas, the trip to Colorado, all the hardships endured, striking it rich, Maxcy as a little tyke, and what a darling boy he was! On and on her mind raced through the events in her life . . .

Augusta could never forget the divorce and losing Horace. Although crushed by the divorce, she still carried the torch for her beloved husband.

"Dear God," prayed Augusta, "Please help me erase my undying love for Horace, from my heart forever."

Could it be that Augusta felt an inward, devastating grip on her heart that would not give her any peace of mind? Within her innermost being, did she feel herself slowly dying of a broken heart?

"I must give up the fight, Horace will never return," thought Augusta. "Life has no purpose for me, and what is there to live for?" mumbled Augusta, turning from side to side. "How lonely and sick I am," she sobbed, as she wrapped a warm shawl around her shoulders.

"Tomorrow is January 31 and would have been our wedding anniversary. Thirty-eight years ago we were married and happy then!" said Augusta in a soft voice.

It was night now, and the city lights were on. These winter days were so short. "It is good to be in a mild climate though," mused Augusta, as she tried to comfort herself.

"Life has been such a struggle," thought Augusta. Tears continued to drop on her pillow . . . oh, so many tears!

Suddenly, breathing became irregular and difficult. Augusta whispered ever so softly to herself, "I just want to sleep . . . sleep . . . sleep . . . sleep "

Later it was discovered that our heroine had passed away in her sleep. At long last, Augusta was at peace.

Maxcy accompanied his mother's remains to Denver, where they were taken to the home of Mrs. T.N. Pierce, located on South Fourteenth Street.

Just as Augusta may have wanted, the services were kept simple. She was buried in a plain black casket, pointed at both ends. A silver plate engraved with her name and age was affixed to the casket. It was impressive as it stood out in prominence on the all-black casket.

Beautiful and touching services were held at the funeral. The casket was placed in the drawing room of Mrs. Pierce, a sister of the deceased, at 2147 Grant Avenue. Relatives and close friends were assembled there, mourning the loss of a honored friend, and one of Colorado's best known women. Rev. N.A. Haskell gave words of consolation quoted from the Bible. Beautiful floral offerings were placed on the casket, and many more filled the room.

At the conclusion of these services, the casket was taken to the Unity Church for the last sad ceremonies. Augusta Tabor was deeply interested in this church and was one of the first members. The lots upon which this ediface was built were a generous gift of Mrs. Tabor. Here again, Rev. N.A. Haskell delivered the touching funeral sermon. The church was crowded to overflowing. Members of the Pioneer Ladies Aid Society occupied the front pews, attending in a body.

Among those present to pay tribute to Mrs. Tabor were pioneers of Denver, the most prominent business men, the members of the church who had worked with Mrs. Tabor during its upbuilding, and men and women best known in society. The church services were brief, but very touching. Many tears were shed at this sad service. The funeral procession was one of the longest ever remembered. A long line of carriages followed the body to the grave in Riverside Cemetery.

All pall bearers were members of the Association of Colorado Pioneers: John L. Dailey, E.F. Hallack, George Tritch, Joseph E. Bates, W.J. Barker and A.G. Rhoads.

148

Mrs. Tabor leaves one child, N. Maxcy Tabor. Other survivors: one brother and five sisters, out of a family of ten children. They are Frank N. Pierce of Tabor, Pierce & Co., Denver; Mrs. R.F. Folsom, Portland, Maine; Mrs. Melvina L. Clarke, Denver; Mrs. Ruth E. Peterson, Augusta, Maine; Mrs. C.L. Marston, Augusta, Maine; and Mrs. C.F. Taylor, Denver.

Two brothers died recently: E.W. Pierce of Denver (5 months before Augusta's death.) F.M. Pierce, in Leadville, died in December, only shortly before Augusta's death.

(Edwin Pierce arrived in Denver in 1876. He boarded at the Grand Central Hotel and sold cigars. He built a home at 2147 Tremont Place in 1879. He had, for a time, owned the Clifton House Hotel at the corner of 17th and Arapahoe streets. After Tabor became Lieutenant Governor, Pierce joined his payroll.)

Newspapers of the day carried the sad story of the death of this great pioneer woman of the West. Her death came as a shock not only to Maxcy and other relatives, but all of Denver mourned her loss.

Maxcy was very close to his mother and faithfully stood by her to the end. At the time of the divorce, he sided with Augusta.

Again, memories of the early days of the country came to mind. Augusta, and other women of pioneer times brought with them, out of the more civilized East, their qualities of culture, education, and refinement. This influence resulted in the great development of Leadville and Denver.

Yes, our dear Augusta had now departed from this life. One by one, the old-time pioneers were lost in death, a sad reality.

Survivors can only be brave and take up life again without their loved ones. It is natural to mourn the death of those dear to us, but we must carry on. Augusta would have wanted it that way. She shall be forever revered on the pages of time and in the hearts of many.

Augusta Tabor's Last Will and Estate: (Her will was filed in County Court.)

The testatrix, after all her just debts are paid, bequeaths to her son Nathaniel Maxy Tabor one-half of her entire estate. She directs that the remaining half be divided equally between her brothers and sisters then living.

She appointed her son, Nathaniel Maxcy Tabor, and her brother, Frank Pierce as executors.

The will closes with this sentence: "This my last will and testament is made without giving my beloved husband Horace A.W. Tabor an interest in the estate of which I die, seized in virtue of the following written consent of him duly signed. Leadville, March 28, 1881.

This is to certify that I give my full consent for my wife to will her property to whomsoever she pleases.

Signed, Horace A.W. Tabor

Witness: Dennis Sullivan

At the time of Augusta Tabor's death, her estate was valued at $1,500,000. It consisted of:

The Tabor mansion on the block on Broadway (opposite the Brown Palace Hotel.)

The corner on which the Hotel Metropole was located.

A block on Lincoln Avenue between 15th and 16th Avenue.

The Golden Eagle Dry Goods property on Lawrence Street.

La Veta Place, residence terrace of twelve houses at Colfax Avenue and South 14th Street.

A number of houses and lots scattered through the city.

Augusta was heavily interested in mines at Leadville.

She was a stockholder in banks in Denver, Gunnison, and other parts of the state.

*Grave stone of Augusta L. Pierce Tabor. Born March 29, 1833, and died on January 30, 1895. She is buried at the Riverside Cemetary in Denver, Colorado. *Note: Tombstone date of 1835 was done in error.*

H.A.W. Tabor funeral as it made its slow journey from the Capitol to Sacred Heart Church and then to its final destination, Mt. Calvary Cemetery. Photo courtesy of the State Historical Society of Colorado.

Evelyn Furman in front of Mrs. Tabor's cabin at the Matchless Mine. 1935.

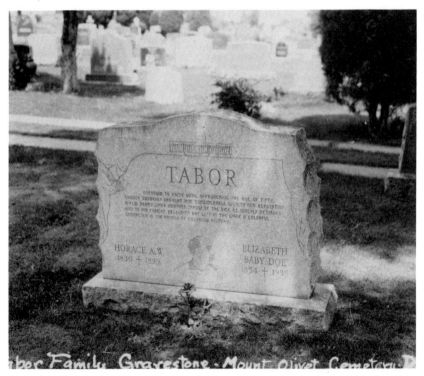

Grave site of Horace and Baby Doe Tabor, Mount Olivet Cemetary, Denver, Colorado.

Chapter Twenty-three
Augusta's Descendants Located

In August 1982, I met Thierry and Janice Perrot at the Tabor Opera House. (They were on tour.) During their visit we became friends, and we still correspond. They were from Guadeloupe, French West Indies. In our conversation about the Tabors, I told them I was in hopes of locating descendants of Augusta Pierce Tabor somewhere in Versailles. Thierry agreed to help me locate the person or persons in France. He soon found Philippe La Forgue, and I am very thankful to Thierry Perrot! I feel greatly indebted to this kind man that did the great favor of locating Augusta's descendants.

Thierry was familiar with France, having lived there previously. I received a letter from Philippe stating that he was one of Persis Augusta Tabor's four children. His letter, in part, reads as follows:

February 14, 1983

Dear Mrs. Furman,

A few weeks ago I received a letter from Mr. Thierry Perrot. This French gentleman says he had made a trip to the United States last August, and had been in touch with you while visiting the Leadville Tabor Opera House.

He says you would like to hear from H.A.W. Tabor's great grand children in France. I must say, I don't know how he succeeded in finding my address, but in fact I am one of Persis Augusta Tabor's four children, and I am very pleased to know that the owner of our grand Opera in Leadville is keen to hear from the descendant of Augusta and Horace.

I have personally spent some time in Denver in 1920, six months in 1929, and have been there only on short visits in 1950 and 1966. Unfortunately, I must say I don't remember having ever seen Leadville although I have been told so many things and have read several books about Leadville Matchless Mine, and Tabor's life.......

I was born in Paris, March 1916, and will soon be 67. Wish I could go back to Colorado sometime with my wife Jeanine, but it is

153

so far from here. Could you send us a few photos of the inside and outside of the Opera House and maybe other interesting things about Leadville?

My mother, Persis Augusta Tabor died in Mallorca, Spain two years ago on January 28th 1987. Have you ever seen the home of my grandparents at 1120 Grant St? It gave me a terrible shock when I was in Denver the last time to see that it had been just torn down. Luckily, I have photos of the home where I enjoyed such wonderful times.

Tell me about yourself. I am very pleased to have heard about you by Mr. Thiery Perrot.

Very sincerely yours,
Phillipe La Forgue

Marie Helen and Jean Michel Conte at St. Cloud, a suburb of Paris, France. Photo by Sharon Krueger, 1985.

Conte Mansion, St. Cloud, a suburb of Paris, France. Evelyn Furman occupied the front bedroom, second floor, right. Photo by Sharon Krueger, 1985.

155

Conte Mansion Children's Theater. Photo by Sharon Krueger, 1985.

Sharon Krueger on the grounds of the Conte Mansion. Photo by Jean Michel Conte, 1985.

Interior of the Conte Mansion, St. Cloud, a suburb of Paris, France. Photo by Evelyn Furman, 1985.

Conte Mansion, Left to Right: Marie Helen Conte, Nathalie Conte and Evelyn Furman. Photo by Sharon Krueger, 1985.

Chapter Twenty-four
Research And A Visit With Friends

I met Marie Helen and Jean Michael Conte in August, 1981. These delightful people had been on tour of the Tabor Opera House, and we became friends. They live in Saint Cloud, a suburb of Paris, France. During our conversation, they suggested that I call them when I went to Paris. "We will show you around," they added. Marie Helen also helped me in my search for the Laforgue family.

In 1985, while on a cruise, I took a side trip to Paris to visit the Conte family. They met me at the airport, and I was delighted to see them again. Soon we arrived at their huge, three-story mansion. I was favorably impressed with all I saw of this stately residence. What a pleasure to be a guest here! Marie Helen gave me a tour of the entire place. I was interested in her family history and in learning more about the house. The interior was elaborately furnished. I admired the French furniture, much of it styled in gold and white. She allowed me to take pictures anywhere, and I was busy with my camera, taking pictures of marble fireplaces, chandeliers, candelabra, clocks, paintings, a grand piano, and sculptures. The grounds were beautifully landscaped. There was a large aviary and two greenhouses (not then in use.) There were garages, a nice home for the gardener, and even a children's theater; a pool, a statue, flower beds, trees, and shrubs to add to the beauty of the grounds. High walls surround the entire property. The iron gates, with grill work, afforded security, (only opened if you knew the combination.) I was taken to a bedroom on the second floor.

"This is your room," said Marie Helen. This stately mansion had beautiful windows with balconies. My room, at the front of the house, was lovely, and I was delighted with the balcony.

I looked out over the grounds, and exclaimed, "Oh, there is the Eiffel Tower in the distance!" In addition to the delicious meals served by the Contes, Marie Helen took time to prepare her specialty dishes and treats for me. The French have good eating. The Contes have a maid to help with the upkeep of this huge mansion. These wonderful friends took me to see the sights of Paris and Versailles. The Chateau in Versailles is a sight to behold! We walked through the acres of grounds surrounding the palace. I was overcome with the beauty of the sculpture, fountains, trees and gardens of flowers. The Trianon, large and small, fascinated me. The French furniture is so beautiful! I had never before seen so much white and gold furniture as is displayed there. One sees remarkable works of art everywhere . . . walls, ceilings, and tapestries! I had heard of this wonderful palace, but it surpassed all my expectations.

The Louvre houses a huge treasure of art. A tour here requires much time if one wants to absorb it all. I enjoyed every minute here.

We took elevators to all levels of the Eiffel Tower . . . didn't miss anything! Then we saw Notre Dame, Arc of Triumph, Invalides, where Napoleon's ashes are. The ashes are placed in a series of six coffins. (Napoleon left an idelible mark on the history of France.) We saw war items displayed in another building.

I felt privileged to think these friends took time from their business to show me the sights. They drove me around many areas and pointed out places of interest one never sees on ordinary tours.

Marie Helen is interested in the theater. She has headquarters in her basement for a little theater group. I was glad that she told me about this, and that she had some famous actors and actresses from other countries coming there. It was interesting to see this area, theater props, and equipment . . . and to learn about their activities. What a talented and clever woman she is, and so remarkable to see how she accomplishes so much. Her husband and their daughters Nathalie and Sandrine added to my times of pleasure during this wonderful visit.

My last night in Paris was something to remember! The Contes arranged a private tour just for me at the Opera Camique. Here they specialize in Opera with spoken dialogue(which is what the term Opera Comique means in French.) Also, a ballet company performs here. This theater was the Royal Palace before the King moved to Versailles, where he built the new palace.

I was guided through long halls lined on each side with sculpture and paintings of the famous people of France. I was delighted with such works of art, and what a happy surprise to have the opportunity to see everything here. I was filled with excitement in seeing the theater. It was all done in red velvet and red carpeting. Yes, I was taken on the grand tour, thanks to the Contes. The private boxes were each supplied with six elegant chairs. Next, I saw the dressing rooms and was taken back stage to see the scenery and props. It was great to see how the stage hands worked the scenery.

The stage was beautiful, and the eighteenth century costumes worn by the actors and actresses were perfect. Their acting was especially good. After the production, I was introduced to the leading man of the opera.

The Contes had arranged a dinner party at a Paris cafe. We were all invited; included were other friends of the Contes.

It seemed that surprises never ended this day! The actor, the leading man, was seated next to me. I enjoyed conversation with the Contes and other guests. The actor was interested in the Tabor Opera House and wanted to know all about it and what is being done there. Before the evening was over, he said, "I will visit your opera house when I next come to your country."

What a great occasion, extending into the late hours. Next morning was bright and beautiful, and we were at the airport.

What wonderful hospitality. I like the French people very much and will treasure memories with these friends always.

With farewells, I was on my way back to the States. As the plane took off, I had my last look at this beautiful country. It was spring, and everything was coming alive . . . "I love Paris in the Springtime."

Philippe and Jeanine Laforgue condominium, Versailles, La Chesnay, France. Photo by Sharon Krueger, 1985.

Part of Phillipe Laforgue's photograph collection. Photo by Sharon Krueger, 1985.

161

Phillipe Laforgue, pictured with his father's World War I sword and other war items. Photo by Sharon Krueger, 1985.

162

Phillipe Laforgue at his desk. Photo by Sharon Krueger, 1985.

Phillipe Laforgue with Evelyn Furman, reviewing Laforgue family photographs, scrapbooks, documents and other historical articles. Photo by Sharon Krueger, 1985.

Phillipe Laforgue with his wife, Jeanine, at their home in LeChesnay, France. Photo by Sharon Krueger, 1985.

Phillipe Laforgue with his wife, Jeanine. Photo by Sharon Krueger, 1985.

164

Phillipe Laforgue with his family photo collection. Photo by Sharon Krueger, 1985.

Dinner at the Philippe Laforgue home. Left to right: Jean Michel Conte, Jeanine Laforgue, Marie Caroline Laforgue, Marie Helen Conte, Philippe Laforgue and Evelyn Furman. Photo by Sharon Krueger, 1985.

Philippe Laforgue stands at the entrance to the beautiful and stately residence of his parents, Paul Alain and Persis, at 122 Avenue Mozart, Paris, France. Their children, Alain, Philippe, Louis and Antoinette, grew up and lived here in their youth. Photo by Sharon Krueger, 1985.

Boyood home of Philippe Laforgue, 122 Avenue Mozart, Paris, France. Photo by Sharon Krueger, 1985.

*Philippe Laforgue and Evelyn Furman enjoying the sights of Paris, France.
Photo by Sharon Krueger, 1985.*

*Dining out in Paris, France, with Philippe and Jeanine Laforgue. Just can't
beat French cooking and the desserts! Photo by Sharon Krueger, 1985.*

167

Dinner at the home of Oliver and Evlyne Laforgue in Versailles, LeChesnay, France. Left to right: Marine Laforgue, Oliver Laforgue, Jeanine Laforgue, Evelyn Furman and Evlyne Laforgue. Photo by Sharon Krueger, 1985.

Sharon Krueger and Evelyn Furman occupied this apartment in Versailles, France, owned by parents of Evlyne Laforgue, while doing research for this book. Photo by Sharon Krueger, 1985.

168

Statue on the grounds of the Chateau, or Palace of Versailles, France. Photo by Sharon Krueger, 1985.

Interior of the Chateau, or Palace of Versailles, France. The King's Study of Louis XV. Photo by Sharon Krueger, 1985.

169

Chateau, or Palace of Versailles, France. Photo by Sharon Krueger, 1985.

Interior of the Chateau, or Palace of Versailles, France. The King's Cabinet or the Council Chamber. Photo by Sharon Krueger, 1985.

170

Sharon Krueger at the Chateau, or Palace of Versailles, France. Photo by Evelyn Furman, 1985.

Interior of the Chateau, or Palace of Versailles, France. Photo by Sharon Krueger, 1985.

Interior of the Louvre, Paris, France. The Venus de Milo. Photo by Sharon Krueger, 1985.

Interior of the Louvre, Paris, France. The Victory of Smathrace, known as the "Winged Victory". Photo by Sharon Krueger, 1985.

172

Chapter Twenty-five
Research and A Visit With The Laforgues

Ivan, son of Oliver and Evlyne Laforgue, visited Leadville in 1984. He was delighted with the Tabor Opera House. He dashed about, filled with excitement, taking pictures throughout the theater. He also visited the Tabor Home owned by Peggy Ducharme. Ivan was delighted to see where his famous ancestors, Augusta and Horace Tabor, once lived. Ivan is their great, great, great grandchild.

On June 16, 1985, I made a second trip to Paris. This was to visit the Laforgue families and to do research for my forthcoming book. My daughter, Sharon Krueger, accompanied me. It was her first trip to France, and she enjoyed this delightful experience. She brought cameras to take pictures needed for my book, which was a great help to me.

Philippe Laforgue met us at the airport. He took us to lovely living quarters in a condominium belonging to some of the family, but vacant at the time of our visit. This would be our headquarters, which was very near his condominium. We were invited to have dinner with the Laforgues, at which time we met Philippe's charming wife Jeanine. We enjoyed our visit, and her French cooking was a real treat.

Philippe still maintains his interior decorating business established in 1979. The decor in their apartment includes priceless heirlooms. We were interested in Philippe's display of swords and military items used by his father Paul Alain Laforgue. (He was an officer in the French Army during World War I.)

Jeanine pointed out a particular large plate hanging on the wall. It is decorated with the initial "N", standing for Napoleon. She is justly proud of this family heirloom. She identified it as once belonging to Napoleon and explained her family connection.

The Laforgues live in a beautiful area. Their living quarters, located in one of many large condominium buildings of this group, is very comfortable. Ample open space is allowed around each building . . . thus a crowding effect is avoided. All buildings are surrounded by attractive landscaped areas. Winding walks lead through green, well-kept lawns. Trees, bushes, and lovely flower gardens give a very attractive effect to the overall picture.

Sharon and I enjoyed other delicious meals as guests of the Laforgues. They gave a special dinner party for us, inviting other family members. We were happy to meet Marie Caroline, a daughter, and also a son, Oliver, and his wife Evlyne. Their children are Ivan, Marine, and Chloe. Also, included guests were Marie Helen and Jean Michel Conte (friends I visited earlier in 1985.)

What a lovely evening, visiting with such special people and another treat of French cooking!

I was anxious to have Sharon see the Conte mansion. We were privileged to go there and have another visit and dinner with the Contes.

I am greatly indebted to these wonderful friends that have done so much for me in so many ways. Another time we were invited to visit Oliver and Evlyne Laforgue and family. We were served a dinner of delicious French cooking and had a fine time. It was good to see their son, Ivan, that visited me in 1984, and he showed us the many photos he took while in Leadville.

The Research

I had long dreamed of the opportunity to do research in France. Now that the Laforgue family had been located, my dream was coming true. Our meeting was a very happy occasion.

Next day, after my arrival, Philippe brought out two suitcases of his family history. "Here are the documents, newspaper clippings, scrapbooks, pictures, and other miscellaneous items I have told you about," said Philippe. His usual smiling face beamed even more than ever as he laid out everything on the table before me.

Philippe then told me how these suitcases might have been lost had he not hid them from the Germans during World War II. He related the troubled times he experienced when the Germans invaded France. The German officials held him in suspicion because of the background of his parents.

Philippe's Father, Paul Alain Laforgue, was born in Sta. Rosalia, Mexico. His mother, Persis Tabor Laforgue, was born in Denver, Colorado, USA. Although Philippe was born in Paris, the Germans questioned his family background and put him in prison. Philippe continued, "I was finally released about the time our twins were born." (Oliver and Gerard are twins of Philippe and Jeanine Laforgue.)

Much time was spent in reading the scrapbooks, newspaper articles and looking over the various items of interest.

After a study of the contents of the suitcases, I copied everything I needed, with Sharon's help. Philippe took me to a place of business

where I could have Xerox copying done, and also to a photographer to
have copies made of rare photographs from the Laforgue collection.

The Laforgues and the good days

One day I asked Philippe about the fortune Maxey had inherited from
Augusta. He answered, "Father lost the money during the depression,
about 1929," Philippe recalled. "I stayed with my grandmother in Denver.
I went back to Paris after Christmas, and then heard the sad news of the
depression."

Philippe, with his mother, father, other brothers and sister, lived in
luxurious living quarters in a fine condominium in Paris. It was located
in the west part of the city: 122 Avenue Mozart, Paris 16th, France. The
family was accustomed to high-class living with a butler and maid.
Philippe took us to see this beautiful building. (Hector Guimard was the
architect and builder.) There are many large three-story buildings in this
area . . . somewhat like huge apartment houses or condominiums.

As we stood looking at the exterior of the second- floor section where
Philippe lived with his family, I noted the beautiful stonework of the
structure. He pointed out the corner section extending on to the back of
the building as their living quarters. "There, about centrally located,
were my rooms," said Philippe. "The ballroom was on third floor," he
added. Then he began to reminisce about the wonderful times he had
there when a young man. (He and his young friends enjoyed a happy
social life.)

The interior was elaborate in design. "Is it still left as it was?" I
asked.

"No," answered Philippe, "Father had it all torn out and
modernized."

After the loss of the fortune during the depression, the family had to
move out of this fine home. The education of the children came to an
abrupt end. "Antoinette had been a medical student and had completed
two years of training," said Philippe. "I had been a law student for two
years," he continued.

Sights of Paris and Versailles

After the research was completed, came the sightseeing of Paris and
Versailles. Now Sharon could see and experience all these sights of the
area (The Contes had already shown me the sights previously, and now I
was seeing it all again with the Laforgues.) It is wonderful to have
friends living in the area to take us on these tours. It is a great advantage
to have them tell us the history and take us to all points of interest not
seen on ordinary tours.

We were filled with wonderment when we visited the Chateau in Versailles. The beauty of it all is breathtaking! The palace had elegant furnishings. Most of the furniture was in white and gold. The wall panels and ceilings were all beautifully painted by famous artists. Richly embroidered fabrics used on bedcovers and draperies are elaborate. Candelabra, chandeliers, clocks of the most beautiful design and workmanship of the masters are displayed. The glitter and brilliance of it all is overwhelming! We spent days of walking and looking. Sharon and I could return here to see it again, as our apartment was walking distance from the Chateau. Hall of mirrors was of outstanding beauty. Ohs! and ahs! were our continual exclamations!

The crowds were so great that Sharon could hardly get positioned with her camera to capture good pictures. Stepping out of the Chateau, we surveyed the gardens which covered many acres. Wide, beautiful avenues of trees, shrubs and sculpture were great to behold. There were pools, canals, and fountains here and there. Flower beds added to the beauty of the grounds. The Grand Trianon and the smaller one were something to remember.

Next we saw the Eiffel Tower, a symbol of Paris. It can be seen from all over the city. We went to the top and enjoyed the view from all directions, looking across the Sein River.

Driving around Paris, one is sure to see the Arc de Triomphe. It was built to celebrate Napoleon's victorious armies. Names of the emperor's many campaigns are carved in this stone arch over the highway.

As we neared Notre Dame we could see the twin towers of this famous Gothic cathedral.

The Louvre is one of the world's major museums. In the 13th Century, it was built as a fortress with towers and high walls. Later, it was the palace of the kings of France. Eventually, the palace was built at Versailles. Now, as a museum, it houses so many treasures, which takes days to see it all! Visitors crowd around the painting of Mona Lisa by Leonardo. Other highlights include: the Victory of Samothrace, known as the Winged Victory, and the Venus de Milo.

The French like to escape the stress of big city life. They work hard and need to get away from the everyday pressure. Many have a second home in some quiet area; it may be a cottage or a converted farm house. The French are known to take the longest holidays in Europe --- it may be six weeks in summer and perhaps another two weeks in winter.

Philippe and wife, the Conte family, and Oliver and family, all have their second residence. Here they can relax and enjoy their holiday.

How grateful I am to the Laforgue family for all the assistance they gave me during my time of research. What a privilege to have access to this treasure-trove of family history. Philippe's help was invaluable!

My research and sightseeing took several weeks. It was all wonderful, and we shall cherish these memories always. What a marvelous visit with the Laforgue families, and their kind hospitality was delightful! My mission in France was now accomplished, and we were homeward bound.

Marine, daughter of Oliver and Evlyne Laforgue, visited me in Leadville in 1986. She enjoyed seeing the Tabor buildings and museums. The rest of the month she spent in Denver with Sharon and family. The following year she returned for another month with Sharon in Denver. Sharon also took her on long trips to other states. Marine likes the United States.

Augusta Louise Pierce -- rare photo, never before published. Courtesy of Philippe Laforgue.

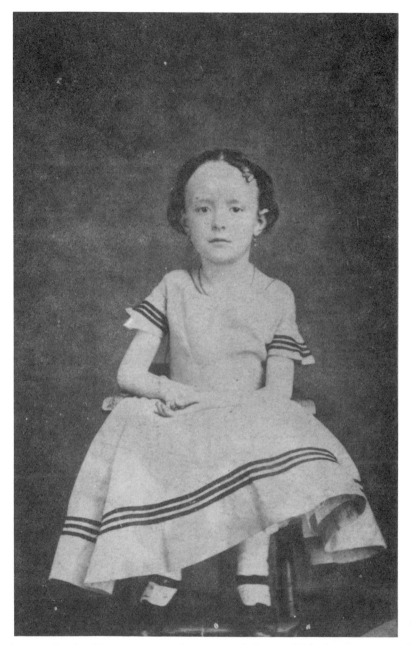

Augusta Louise Pierce -- rare photo, never before published. Courtesy of Philippe Laforgue.

Augusta Louise Pierce -- rare photo. Courtesy of Philippe Laforgue.

Chapter Twenty-six
Following The "Silver Star"
And Ending The Tabor Dream

The saga of Augusta Pierce Tabor reads like a drama of the Old West! Her life unfolds dramatically from its beginning to its ending. In fact, her life story would make a great stage production, movie, or television show.

The interlude between our heroine's childhood in Augusta, Maine, and her death in Pasadena, California is filled with touching and exciting events.

In tracing the lives of Augusta and Horace from New England to Kansas, we learn how they are caught up in the fever of excitement of the Pike's Peak gold rush. These early pioneers endured perilous times of hardships and danger in their search for gold. Thus, Augusta suffered through all these trials and tribulations in her life on the rough frontier. She washed the family clothes in the cold water of the mountain streams. Often she washed miners' clothes to earn money. She cooked over campfires, nursed sick and injured miners, opened a bakery, and took in boarders. Money she earned in this way often kept the family and even paid for the Kansas farm. She helped with the farming and also mining. She was both storekeeper and postmistress, always filling in wherever needed. In spite of all the hardships, Augusta and Horace, with other gold seekers, forged ahead.

Miners and prospectors, met along the way, were shocked to see a woman roughing it in this rugged mountain country. Augusta was the first white woman in the area.

In review, consider the Tabor journey through South Park to California Gulch. Here they experienced dangerous times, fording the rivers. Augusta, in her diary, writes of one occasion when the oxen were so thin, weak, and tired that they halted in the middle of the river and could go no farther. The men plunged into the ice cold water and tried to drag them along. The wagon had to be unloaded and goods placed on ice, which might break loose at any moment. What a hazardous ordeal to undergo in order to cross a river!

Mention is made again of another fording of the river: The wagon bed raised above the wheels and floated down the stream with Augusta and child in it. It was rapidly filling with water. Augusta clung to the willows on the bank until the men came to the rescue. She knew nothing more until they were at the mouth of California Gulch. She and young Maxcy nearly lost their lives this time. This was one of Augusta's most perilous experiences. It is amazing that she lived to tell the story.

I am impressed with Augusta's courage and presence of mind in grabbing the willows and clinging fast to all there was for her to seize. With death at the door, Augusta had unbelievable strength and held out until the men were able to come to the rescue. She was determined to save her child, and what a miracle that they both escaped death!

The Tabors follow their "Star of Silver" to California Gulch, Oro and later Leadville. Thus, the next part of the story is set at a faster pace. Here Augusta is kept busy with the store and post office. She persevered. She was always the devoted wife and stuck by Horace through "thick and thin." Always keeping the dream of good times, they did strike it rich! Fortune smiled upon the Tabors, and soon they were worth nearly ten million!

Horace spent most of his fortune building up Leadville and Denver. He was a big spender, but Augusta remained the frugal one. Riches brought marital separation. Augusta was unhappy and lonely because they were drifting apart. Then came the divorce after Baby Doe arrived upon the scene. Horace married Baby Doe, and Augusta was crushed. This turn of events was Augusta's darkest hour, and her world was falling apart.

Thinking back, it is evident that without Augusta, Horace might not have struck it rich.

During the panic of 1893, Horace lost his fortune. Augusta invested her money wisely and increased her fortune. Still carrying the torch for Horace, she looked forward to the day when he might return to her. He never did come back.

She even offered to help him financially after he lost everything. He refused her help, as his pride restrained him. Augusta died with a broken heart in 1895 --- a millionaire! She left her fortune to their son Maxcy and her brothers and sisters then living. Horace died in 1899. At his bedside was Maxcy (son of Augusta and Horace); also two daughters of Baby Doe and Horace, (Lily and Silver.)

Maxcy and his family lived a normal life without being touched by tragedy. Lily, the older daughter of Horace and Baby Doe, married her cousin, had children, and lived a fairly good life. Apparently, Lily chose to disassociate from the Tabor connection in Colorado, and none of her descendants have come forward to claim identification. Silver, on the other hand, the younger daughter, came to a tragic end in Chicago. She died under mysterious circumstances --- a drug addict and alcoholic.

After the Tabor fortune was lost, Baby Doe ended up in an old shack at the Matchless Mine. She guarded the mine with hopes that the Matchless would pay millions again. She lived in poverty, alone with her memories. She was found dead in her mountain abode in 1935.

The Tabor fortune brought comfort, enjoyment, and good things to many of the Tabor relatives and friends. Large donations were made to any deserving cause. Tabor wealth built up the cities of Leadville and Denver . . . also other parts of Colorado. It was gratifying to the Tabors to see the good that their money did for many worthwhile causes. Augusta made large donations to churches and church organizations. She was always ready to help the needy.

Alas, fame and fortune did not bring lasting happiness to Augusta or Horace. How sad. Of all sad words of tongue or pen, the saddest are these: "It might have been!" (John Greenleaf Whittier)

In retrospect, once again we have evaluated the accomplishments of Augusta. It is amazing what this great pioneer woman could do under the circumstances of the time, and often single-handedly. Augusta was an inspiration to all with whom she came in contact. Her key to success was perseverance!

Augusta's way of life and her other values exemplify her many good qualities of character. She has been justly recognized as an outstanding pioneer woman. May her life of perseverance continue on as an inspiration to future generations. The memory of Augusta will live in our hearts forever. Augusta's descendants may rightfully be very proud of their ancestor, Augusta Pierce Tabor!

I have tried to relate my observations in France as to how Augusta's descendants are faring. Photos taken there are meant to show that they are happy and contented.

The Tabor story is so famous that many on tour with me, at the Tabor Opera House, ask, "Where are the Tabor descendants, and what are they doing?" Some of the Tabor fans have even asked this question: "What about the Tabor fortune that Augusta left?"

It was delightful to visit Augusta's descendants in their beautiful area, an area surrounded by art and culture. I was favorably impressed with the historical buildings and museums, all housing world-famous works of art. The Louver, with fine sculptures and paintings by the Masters, is overwhelming. How wonderful to have the Palace of Versailles with all its treasures at your finger tips! So much to see of beauty and historical significance.

Augusta traveled abroad and knew about many of the Wonders of the World. If she could see her descendants now, I think she would be satisfied that "all is well."

It has been a joy to research the life and times of our heroine Augusta Pierce Tabor. With the help of new-found friends along the way of my research and travels, the story continued to unfold beautifully.

This thorough hunt for information has proven very rewarding and even exciting. All the facts I had hoped to find were revealed, and even more.

In conclusion, the curtain comes down on the story of that remarkable woman --- Augusta Pierce Tabor, Leadville's first lady!

THE "SILVER STAR"
By Sharon Furman Krueger

THE "SILVER STAR" WAS A DREAM . . .
IN THE HEARTS OF MAN AND WIFE.
A CONQUERING OF THE NEW FRONTIER . . .
FILLED WITH STORMS AND STRIFE.

TOGETHER, WITH FIRM RESOLUTION . . .
BREAKING A TRAIL TO THE WEST.
HEADS HELD HIGH IN THE STORMS . . .
WITH HARDLY A MINUTE OF REST.

A SON BORN IN THE WILDERNESS. . .
ALONE, NO COMFORTS OF HOME.
LONELY, FRIGHTENED, EXHAUSTED . . .
LISTENING TO THE STORMS WINDY DRONE.

BUT THE "SILVER STAR" WAS SHINING . . .
FILLING THEIR HEARTS WITH DREAMS AND HOPE.
THEY MADE IT TO COLORADO . . .
THE JOURNEY HAD TAUGHT THEM TO COPE.

DECISIONS OF DREAMER AND REALIST . . .
RESULTED IN GLITTER AND GOLD.
THROUGH BALANCE OF TWO HEARTS TOGETHER . . .
TABOR'S FAME AND RICHES UNFOLD.

BUT THE "STAR OF SILVER" GREW TARNISHED . . .
WITH RICHES, THERE'S OFTEN A PRICE.
THE WEDGE BETWEEN THEM WAS DRIVEN . . .
FOR HIM, WOULD HIS FIRST WIFE SUFFICE?

'GUSTA HAD WEATHERED THE STORM . . .
PERSEVERANCE AND COURAGE UNTOLD.
BUT THE "STAR OF SILVER" WAS NOTHING . . .
WITHOUT HER HUSBAND, TO HOLD.

A WOMAN, WHO COULD BE HER CHILD . . .
WAS NOW IN THE ARMS OF HER MAN.
BUT SHE FOUGHT WITH PREVAILING PERSISTENCE . . .
HER ATTITUDE WAS STILL THAT . . . "I CAN!"

AND SHE DID CONQUER ALL PUT BEFORE HER . . .
BEFORE THE "STAR" FADED, AND FELL.
BUT NOW, HER LIFE WAS SHATTERED . . .
IN THE DEPTHS OF A COLD, DARKENED WELL.

THE "SILVER STAR" HAD BUILT UP CITIES . . .
BUT HAPPINESS, IT COULD NOT BUY.
PERSEVERANCE HAD BROUGHT THEM GLORY . . .
BUT NOW SHE WANTED TO DIE.

185

"GUSTA, THIS FRONTIER LADY . . .
LEAVES US WEALTH, THAT SILVER CAN'T BUY.
HER "GUSTO" AND LOVE FOR OTHERS . . .
MOTIVATES US TO "NEVER SAY DIE!"

THAT'S WHAT FRONTIERS ARE MADE OF . . .
GO AHEAD, FOLLOW YOUR DREAM!
LIFE IS NOT MADE OF COMFORT . . .
BUT OF COURAGE AND SELF-ESTEEM.

APPENDIX A
Gravestones in Wall Cemetery

Bette joined Mike and me and directed us to the Wall Cemetery, where she showed us the graves of her family. First grave we saw was that of a stone marked Father Abel B.
(Babcock) Pierce Died Sept. 3, 1893 Et. 83 yrs. Bette said this was her great grandfather. Next grave stone was marked Mother Mary A. wife of Abel B. Pierce died May 16, 1881. Et 71 yrs. Next row directly in front of these graves marked as Oliver A. died Oct. 13, 1816 Et. 9 years and beside this was another marked Adeline V (Viola) Died Oct. 12,18 . . . at 5 years 9 mo. children of Abel and Mary A. Pierce.

Next, we were taken to Ben Venue Cemetery: A grave stone marked Father Horace H. Pierce , May 8, 1843   Dec. 23, 1913   Hattie L. Pierce May 11, 1858, Oct. 15, 1924 wife of Horace H. Pierce
Other stones marked as follows:
Pierce, Walter S. 1892-1965
Pierce, Lillian Emma 1901-1973
Edward Israel Pierce 1899-1973 (brother of Walter S. Pierce)
George W. Verrill Aug. 17, 1882 - May 12, 1956
Leona Pierce Verrill May 15, 1889 - Oct. 13, 1947
(Leona was a sister of Walter S. Pierce)
Gladys H. Pierce - sister of Walter S. Pierce 1897-
I took pictures of the graves, as I try to keep a record of all Pierces I find; I am also doing a search on my branch of Pierce history. I am not sure these are the Pierce names I am seeking, but have recorded it all in my notebook for future reference.

APPENDIX B
Augusta's Complete Genealogy

From Pierce Genealogy being the record of the posterity of John Pers, an early inhabitant of Watertown, in New England, who came from Norwich, Norfolk County , England.
By Frederich Clifton Pierce, Esq. 1880
Thomas Weston was associated with Pierce in this enterprise, and both were doubtless men of influence in those days. John Peirce's son, Richard Pierce was a resident of Pemaquid, or rather Muscongus, and married Elizabeth Brown. Richard Pierce's children were Richard, William, Joseph, Elizabeth who m. Richard Fulworth, George, Margaret who m. Nathaniel Ward, and Francis.

Genealogy of the Pierce Family given to the author by Horace Howell Pierce.
THE PIERCE FAMILY
By the tenth century, social conditions were such that it was becoming increasingly complex and specialized. Population increased, new economic and political systems were developed. It became obvious that a single name was not sufficient for purposes of identifying people. Thus, the use of hereditary surnames (or

187

family names which are passed down to later generations in the same or similar form) began to find common acceptance.

People took as surnames the names of flowers (Lilly, Rose), fish (Herring, Pike), animals (Fox, Bears), birds (Peacock, Swan), and place names (Hill, Wood, Field, Town). Another source was occupations, such as (Taylor, Potter, Smith, Sadler, Carpenter, Brewer, and others).

Still others chose the names of their fathers as surnames. Thomas James meaning simply, Thomas, the son of James. There was a time in English history when no one would dare to use a Biblical name; it was considered to be highly disrespectful. Old barriers were broken down, and became fashionable to pick a child's name from the Bible. The names of the apostles were favorites.

The name Pierce is one of many names which evolved from the word Peter, Piers. Other variants are: Pearce, Pears, Pearse, Pieris, Peers, Peirs, Perse, Peres, Perris, Pierse, and others.

When considered as one group, Pierce and the other variants of Piers are common names in present day England, especially in the southern countries. But, when we consider Pierce alone, we find that members of the family are concentrated principally in the North Wales and Sussex.

1. John Pers (Pierce) m. Elizabeth
b. 1588 d. 8/18/1661 in England b. 1591 d. 3/12/1666/7

Emigrated from Norwick, Norfolk County, England in 1637, either on board the ship "John and Dorethey" of Norwick, or the "Rose of Yarmouth". Mr. William Andrews Sen. was Master of the former, and his son the latter vessel.

Weaver, age 49 years and Elizabeth aged 35 years with children, John, Barbre, Elizabeth and Judeth.

John was grantee of one lot in Watertown, Mass. and purchaser of three lots, before 1644, one of which was his homestead of 12 acres. Was admitted freeman in 3/1638. (Which means; generally, these emigrants were people in early middle life, possibly married with a few children. Their passage was financed by indenture, a system of quasi-slavery in which they offered up to seven years of service to a colonial master for payment of their fare). Was Deputy to the General Court 1638/39. A man of good estate. 8 children, the four who came with their parents, John, Elizabeth (m. John Ball Jr.), Judeth (m. Francis Wyman 1/30/1645), Barbre (may have died on the way over). Four who came before their parents, *Anthony, Esther (m. Joseph Morse Jr.) Robert (m. Mary Knight), Mary (m. Coldum). In John's will of 1661 named spelled Perse, in Elizabeth's will 4/2/1667 name spelled Pearse.

2. Anthony, son of John (I) m. Mary . . . in Eng.d.1633 in Mass.
b.in Eng.1609 d 5/9/1678 2dm 1633 Ann in Mass d.1/20/1682/3

He was admitted freeman 9/3/1634 in Salem, settled in Watertown, Mass.in 1649. 9 children John, Mary, Mary (if a child died young, sometimes, gave a latter child the same name), Jacob, Daniel, Martha, *Joseph, Benjamin, and Judith. In Ann's will, name spelled Peirce.

3. Joseph, son of Anthony (2) m. Martha
b.probably 1647 d.1701 2dm.6/15/1698 Mrs. Elizabeth Kendall Winship
Resided in Watertown   b. in Woburn MASS. 1/15/1652

10 children Joseph, Francis, *John, Mary, Benjamin, Jacob, Martha, Stephen, Israel, and Elizabeth.

4. John, son of Joseph (3) m. Elizabeth Smith
b5/27/1673 d.1743/4   11/4/1702 b.1/15/1702
Resided in Waltham & Watertown, MASS.

7 children *John Jr., Jonas, Ezekiel, Samuel, Elizabeth, Daniel & Jonathon.

5. John Jr., son of John (4) m. Rebecca Fenno
b.9/1/1703 d.3/3/1774 3/4/1731 b.9/8/1697 d.3/3/1783

Weaver, resided in Watertown, latter moved to Stoughton. In his will probated 3/25/1774, name is spelled Pierce.
Rebecca is granddaughter of John Fenno of Lancashine, England. Emigrated to Milton, MASS. B. 1629 d.4/7/1708
5 children *Eliphalet, Seth, Elizabeth, (m.Smith) Abigail (m. Tilden), & John.
6. Eliphalet, son of John Jr. (5) m. Elizabeth Wheeler
b.7/29/1728 d.8/1798   3/12/1755 b.2/22/1732/3 d.1/1798
Resided in Stoughton, MASS, moved to Augusta, ME. about 1784.   Purchased a farm on River Road, now Riverside Drive. Both buried on part of farm, which is now Wall Cemetery.
12 children Eliphalet & William, whom went to MASS. & N.Y., Samuel (m. Lucy Fuller), Isaiah, John, Elizabeth (m. Daniel Savage), Jason b.5/15/1770 (m. Prudence Price), *Asa (m. Mehitable Babcock), Mehitable (m. Samuel Babcock, brother to Mehitable Babcock), Sarah (m. Ballard), Hannah (m. Trask). another daughter (m. Getchell).
7. Asa, Son of Eliphalet (6) m Mehitable Babcock
b. 1780 d.12/1860 10/22/1803 b. 1/6/1778 7 children * Abel Babcock, William (m. Lucy Eaton), Jefferson (m. Ruth Clark), Newell (m. Ann M. Stackpole), Vesta (m. Wm. Getchell), Tabatha m. Pitts & Daly), Johann (m. Alfred Turner).
8. William Babcock Pierce
b. Oct 20, 1804 d. March 27, 1873 m. Nov 13, 1828 Lucy S. Eaton (Pierce) b. June 10, 1805 d. May 22, 1875
Children of William Babcock Pierce and Lucy S. Eaton Pierce:
Rebecca Foster
b. August 27, 1829 m. P.J. Folsom Feb 22, 1852 d. Jan 9, 1899
Lucy Melvina
b. April 28, 1831 m. Arthur C. Clark Mar 30, 1861 d. Aug 2, 1896
Louisa Augusta
b. Mar 29, 1833 m. Horace A.W. Tabor Jan 31, 1857 d. Jan 30, 1895
Vesta
b. Jan 13, 1835 d. May 30, 1855
Ruthe Elizabeth
b. Sept 29, 1836 m. F.D. Peterson Nov. 6, 1865 d. Sept 1, 1907
William Henry (Edwin)
b. Sept 26, 1838   m. Frances Irene Saben May 28, 1859 d. Dec 25, 1894
Nahum Franklin
b. July 2, 1840 m. Flora E. Moody Jan 19, 1871 d. Mar 17, 1909
Mary Frances
b. Apr 15, 1842 m. Charles L. Marston June 28, 1862 d. June 10, 1899
Lilla Taylor
b. Apr 22, 1844 m. C. F. Taylor of Narridgewock Feb. 13, 1867 d. May 16, 1925
Freddie Marshall
b. June 23, 1846 m. Mary L. Yeaton Jan 4, 1873 d. Sept 10, 1894
10 children
9. Louisa Augusta Pierce m. Horace A.W. Tabor
b. March 29, 1833 Jan 31, 1857 married b. Nov. 26, 1830
daughter of Wlliam Babcock Pierce / son of Cornelius Dunham Tabor
1 child Nathaniel Maxcy
10. Nathaniel Maxcy Tabor   m.   Luella Babcock
b Oct 9, 1857 / daughter of J.D. Babcock
1 child Persis Augusta Tabor

11. Persis Augusta Tabor b. May 29, 1894 - Brown Palace Hotel, Denver, Colo. d Jan 28, 1981 in Palena Mallorca, Spain m Feb 24, 1914 Paul Alien Laforgue. b. Apr. 17, 1889d Aug 24, 1938 in Paris
    Son of Charles Louis Laforgue
    4 children Alain, Louis, Jacques Philippe, Antoinette
  12. Jacques Philippe Laforgue b. March 11, 1916 m. Sept. 17, 1943 M. Jeanine Children Oliver, Gerard (twins) Marie Caroline
    Children of Philippe and Jeanine Laforgue:
    13. Oliver wife Evlyne
    Children: Ivan, Marine, Chloe
    13. Gerard Wife Marie France
    Children Valerie, Isabel, Pierre, Philippe
    Marie Caroline-Not married
    Note: Oliver and Gerard are twins

    This ends the complete genealogy of Augusta Pierce Tabor and her family.

    For the benefit of any readers interested in the rest of the Horace Howell Pierce genealogy, it is continued as follows:
  7. Asa, son of Eliphalet (6)
  b. 1780 d. 12/1860 m. 10/22/1803 Mehitable Babcock b. 1/6/1778
  7 children Abel Babcock, *William m Lucy Eaton, Jefferson m. Ruth Clark Newell m. Ann M. Stackpole, Vesta m Wm. Getchell, Tabatha m. Pitts and Daly, Johann m. Alfred Turner
  8. Able, son of Asa (7) m. Mary Ann Gardner
  b. 7/8/1810 d.9/3/1893   b. 1810 d.5/16/1881
  Farmer and Stone Cutter.   Both buried in Wall Cemetery
  6 children, all born in Augusta
  Oliver Alonzo b. 1837 d. 10/13/1846 Buried Wall Cemetery
  Eliza Jane b. 1839 m. Summer Merrill
  Adeline V. b. 1/28/1841 d.10/12/1846 Buried Wall Cemetery
  Adelaide V. b. 1/28/1841 d.8/19/1921 Buried Wall Cemetery
   m. Geroge E. Hewins B. 1827 d. 10/18/1892 Buried Wall Cemetery
  *Horace Hampton F.
  Elizabeth b. /19/1845
  9. Horace Hampton, son of Abel (8)
  b.5/3/1843 d.12/23/1913
Was in 'Who's Who' as a prominent farmer and cattle dealer. A boulder on River bank by Fort Western, with a plaque in memory of B. Arnold and his troops, stopping at the Fort on way to Quebec, came from Pierce farm.
    Horace and Hattie are buried in Bien Venue Cemetery, Augusta 9 children all born in Augusta.
    Lydia J. Pierce m. 7/4/1872 b.1845 Vassalboro, ME. d. 2/5/1889 daughter of Geo. W. and Mariam Cross Pierce, granddaughter of Pelatiah & Hannah Whitehouse Pierce m. 12/22/1803 in Berwick, ME. Lydia buried Cross Hill cemetery, Vassalboro.
    Hattie Lucinda Bean b. 5/11/1858 in Jay, ME. d. 10/15/1924 daughter of Isaac B. & Mary Elizabeth Goding (m. 4/4/1855) Bean. Teacher, also played organ in church and sang.
    Horace Hampton m. Hattie Lucinda Bean 2dm.
  9. children of Horace Hampton
  (10) George Edward
  b. 2/18/1874 d.1/1/1957

Farmer & Self Employed
married Elizabeth Jones Haskell
b.2/19/1883 d.1963
Teacher Both Buried Mt. Hope Cemetery
(10) Viola Addie
b.5/30/1874 d.4/11/1901
Married Charles D. Jones
b. 1/27/1870, Starks Resided in Windsor
(11) Charles Elroy Jones
b. 5/7/1899 in Windsor d.4/14/1968 m. Sadie
Self employed in West Haven, CT
Married 2 Margaret Kasnlis B Minnusville PA 4/23/07
Buried in Rest Haven Cemetery, Windsor.
(10) Horace Arthur
b 9/23/1881 d. 8/16/1960
Baker
Both buried St. Mary's Cemetery, (Green St.) Augusta
    4 children 3 born in Augusta
Married 8/4/1908 Augusta Mary Ann Howell b. 5/12/1885 Johnsville N.B.
    Canada d.4/16/1967 Daughter of George & Mary Donovan Howell
(11) Horace Howell
b. 12/25/1909 in Livermore Falls
Textile & school employee
2 daughters born in Augusta
Anita Lillian Cloutier. m. 10/14/1939
b. 12/12/1917 Augusta
Daughter of Augustine & Angeline Cloutier
Fancy Stitcher
(12) Joan May - office worker
b.5/10/1940
Married Eugene Fred Haskell, 6/11/1960
b.1/14/1936, Augusta
I.B.M. operator
2 sons born in Augusta
(13) Steven Pierce Haskell b. 3/22/1962 m. Lisa Lindsay Son Cole -3/1984
 Gregory Eugene Haskell b. 5/26/1966 (James B. 2dm Painter) b. Peery, MO
    Elec. Tech.   1/20/1937

(12) Wanita June	m.	Thomas Frances Meagher
b. 6/24/1941	Augusta	b. 12/12/1939 in Augusta
Secretary	9/9/1961	School Superintendent
3 children		
(13) Timothy James Meagher		b. 11/26/1964 in Lewiston, Me.
Karen Ann Meagher		b. 5/19/1966 in Lewiston, Me.
David Howell Meagher		b. 8/19/1969 in Brunswick, Me.
(11) Alvin Wilfred	m.	Luise Rank of Germany
b. 3/31/1913 d. 6/9/1971	5/1956 in Germany	
World War II Veteran 20 yr. Army Retiree		
Buried Fort Sam Houston National Cemetery, Texas		
(11) Leo Maynard	m.	Kathleen Mary McArthur
b.11/28/1916	5/8/1941	12/8/1912 Prince Edward Island
Cook & store clerk Augusta		Waitress
(11) Mary Leola	m.	Forest Philip Vigue
b.1/4/1920	9/7/1940	b.10/27/1912 Skowhegan, Me.
Gates Buss. School	Augusta	Central Maine Power Co, retiree

4 children b. Augusta
(12) Janice Ann   m.   40 years working head lineman
b.1/19/1942   5/16/1964   Robert Shelton Howe
Secretary   Augusta   b.11/13/1939
(13)Robert Michael Howe   b.4/22/1965 Comptroller, Central Me. Power
Stephen William Howe   b.3/19/1967
(12) Philip Brian Vigue   b.12/27/1945 Accountant (State)
Susan Marie Vigue   b.11/9/1949
Patricia Mary Vigue   b.8/12/1962
(10) Leigh Ellsworth   m.   Mildred Fish Smith
b.2/22/1884   d.10/21/1977   b.10/6/1883 d.1933
Electirc car conductor   2d m.   Kathleen Geary b.2/9/1883
State employee 26 yrs   buried Bien Venue Cemetery
One son b. Augusta
(11) Kenneth Leland
b.11/26/1916 U.S. Navy   Mechanical engineer
(10) Leona Mary   m. George W. Verrill
b.5/15/1889   d. 10/13/1947   b. 8/17/1882(Portland) d.5/15/1956
Teacher.   Owner and operator of Augusta Print Shop.
                                Both buried Bien Venue Cemetary.

(10) Walter Sherman   m.   Lillan Emma Brawm
b.6/10/1892 d.12/21/1965   b.5/31/1901 Lisbon Falls
Self-employed & mill worker   Bookkeeper   d.1/23/1973
Both buried Bien Venue Cemetery   dau. of Harry & Lillian Bowen Brawn
5 children born in Augusta
(11) Hattie Mae b. 4/18/1925 d. 4/18/1925
(11) Lillian Elizabeth   m. Braley
b.8/3/1926
Teacher (master's degree)
(12) one dau. Darlene
(11) Celinda Lou
b.10/29/1928
R.N. Nurse, also U.S. Nurse (Navy)
(11) Beverley Joyce   m.   Theodroe Langdon Roess
b.3/14/1930   Engineer
Nurse with advance degrees
3 children
        (12)   Deborah Anne   b.6/11/1952
               Douglas Allan   b.11/16/1954
               Derek Langdon   b.1/10/1957   d.5/18/1975

(11) Walter Sherman
b.11/4/1931   Self employed & construction
(10) Elizabeth (Peggy) Lora   m.   Thomas F. Glynn
b.11/4/1894   d.7/3/1974   6//16/1939   b.11/9/1884 d.9/12/1952
Teacher   Mass.   Proprietor of Diner, Lowell,Mass
Both buried at St. Patrick's Cemetery, Lowell, Mass.
(10) Gladys Hampton
b.7/2/1897   Was a prominent local golfer & bowler.
Bookkeeper I.R.S. 21 years retiree.
(10) Israel Gardner   m.   Dorothy Greenfield
Changed name to   N.Y.
Edward Israel   2d. m Ethel Doney

192

b.6/26/1899 d.11/4/1973   8/4/1949   Teacher
Athletic Director & Coach
Cony High, Augusta & Ithaca, N.Y.   Boston Red Sox's Scout
Buried Bien Venue Cemetery, Augusta, Me.
2 daughters
(11) Virginia Keeler   b.8/30/1932   d. 1948
(11) Linda Jean Greenfield   m. Dirk Koopman
      b.12/28/1937   b. in Holland
      3 children   Engineer
(12) Nineke
      Pieter
      Katrina

APPENDIX C
More About The Risches

Mr. and Mrs. Richard Parshall (Anabel) of Old Greenwich, Conn. went on tour of the Tabor Opera House in October 1981. Mrs. Parshall told me that she owned a sterling silver tea strainer that once belonged to Augusta Tabor. (There was a light gold wash inside of the bowl.) She agreed to send me a picture of it, and it is reproduced for this book. (This was a gift from her Aunty Rische, better known as Grace.) Anabel's father had foster parents, Grace & Ernest Rische. Augusta used this tea strainer when entertaining important guests.

Anabel says, "The Tabor story was one I heard many times in my childhood. In 1936 we went to San Antonio Texas to visit "Aunty Rische" (Grace). The tea strainer was given to Anabel at this time - 1936.

Anabel's father mentioned that Ernest Rische was manager of the San Antonio Opera House. Her grandfather was an orchestra conductor and traveled too much to provide a home for my father. Finding the Risches was a fortunate part of my father's childhood.

Anabel sent me a xerod copy of a letter her father wrote. He is reviewing the story of the Risches and Tabors (contained in the Rische history). It reads as follows:

"The following background of my foster parents, the Risches, may be of interest to you. Auntie Rische was born in Lewiston, Maine. Her maiden name was Grace Babcock. Her father was editor of the Lewiston Sentinal. Her cousin married and settled in Leadville, Colorado where her husband ran a country general merchandise store.

It was the custom, in those days, for a storekeeper to grubstake prospectors. Mr. Rische's uncle and a miner named Hook were in a grubstake partnership with the storekeeper, H.A.W. Tabor. Their claim became a bonanza (The Little Pittsburgh Silver Mine) and they all became millionaires.

Tabor moved to Denver, built the Tabor Opera House, the lobby being encrusted with silver dollars. This was about the time the country went on the silver standard.

Rische's nephew Ernest came to visit his uncle and met Mrs. Tabor's cousin (auntie Rische) Grace Babcock and married her. Her old photos proved her to have been a very beautiful woman. Tabor went wild with his money, divorced his wife and married Baby Doe, a dance hall girl. He died broke, and his last wife went to live in an old shack near the mine, hoping that it would again produce. She died about 1935 of starvation and cold, friendless and alone.

Auntie Rische, after her marriage, went to her husband's home in San Antonio, Texas."

193

APPENDIX D
More About Maine

Since Augusta Pierce Tabor was a native of Maine, I am interested in learning more about the state, and how it may have influenced her background.

In review, I have gathered some interesting facts about Maine for extra reading. Observations made personally while I was in Augusta and the surrounding area I feel worthy of mention are in the following account:

Thousands of Indians lived in Maine before the coming of the white man. It is believed that Leif Erickson led the Vikings to Maine about 1000 A.D.

English pioneers first settled in Maine in 1607 (13 years before the Pilgrims landed in Plymouth Rock.) They returned to England the next year because of cold weather and lack of supplies. In the 1620's, the English returned and made permanent settlements. Maine was part of Massachusetts for about 200 years.

Pilgrims from Plymouth Colony in Massachusetts built the first trading post called Cushnoc in 1628. Augusta is located on this site. Fort Western was built on the site of the old trading post in 1754. The settlements surrounding the Fort were part of Hallowell. In 1797, Hallowell and Augusta were separated and Augusta became the Capital in 1832.

In North's history on Augusta, we learn that bridges were continually being destroyed by the ice and flood waters that swept down the river valley. Time after time the bridges, dams and locks were rebuilt.

Population increased, and agriculture, commerce, and manufacturing developed. River and ocean navigation prospered. Steamer traffic on the river ended with the coming of the railroad.

Mike took me on drives around Augusta and Hallowell. Augusta is located at the head of the Kennebec River. The bridge across the river immediately caught my eye. The city has a beautiful setting here in the rolling hills of the area. Many trees all through the city add to the picturesque scene. Standing at a vantage point above Augusta, I look over the hillside and valleys. The homes and other buildings nestled among the trees on various street levels of the entire hillside stand out to advantage. I noticed grey stone buildings on a hill. I was told this is the arsenal built in 1828. Public buildings then were the State House, State insane asylum and U.S. Arsenal.

We drove through the industrial center on the west side of the river. Mike pointed out one large building and said it was once a shoe factory. It was closed down permanently, as are the textile industries. Now, imported merchandise at lower prices has put these factories out of business. The depression of the 1930's created hardships. Farming almost came to an end.

Mike told me about the ice industry in Maine; ice was cut and shipped to Europe. Entire shiploads went across the waters. The return trip brought goods for United States from Europe. Modern refrigeration replaced this industry also.

Looking at the map of Maine, one can see the unpopulated area in the North. Ninety percent of Maine is covered by forests. In the wilderness there are animals such as bear, deer and moose. Tyke Mollay said the moose have sometimes been known to walk across the road in downtown Augusta, which delights the tourists.

There are still many trees around Church Hill Road. The thick growth of underbrush makes an ideal home for smaller animals. Ernest Richardson mentioned hearing coyotes near his home at night, catching rabbits. He described the noise of the chase and the gruesome, and last eerie shriek of the captured rabbit.

Pine Tree State is the nickname for Maine. The pine has tall and straight trunks that make the best masts for sailing vessels. Until the late 1700's, Maine's greatest resource was the pine tree, but now most of the trees are second growth.

Mike took me to Portland. There are many finger-like peninsulas, and Portland is on a mile-wide peninsula; it has a fine harbor. Maine is deeply cut and indented by bays and inlets. Here is the nearest U.S. port to Europe. What a perfect fortress! Mike said it was ideal for use in time of war; a good place for a U.S. Naval station. This location was the best on the whole Atlantic coast.

I enjoyed a drive around Portland harbor. Mike pointed out large islands usually owned by wealthy people. The picturesque lighthouses drew my attention. I was especially interested in the Old Port Exchange District on the waterfront, which has been restored to Victorian style. Walking up and down the streets, we wandered in and out of the shops. (Mike had lived around this area during his boyhood days.) I was delighted to hear about his memories of the area. We investigated a large, old brick building now restored. Here, we had lunch in a restaurant on the second floor. We had a table by a window and could observe people on the Victorian streets below. I enjoyed the food and Victorian atmosphere.

Wadsworth Longfellow's house in Portland is Maine's most popular historic site. This is the boyhood home of Henry Wadsworth Longfellow, the famous poet.

Another interesting trip was when Mike took me to Brunswick, Maine. He wanted me to see Bowdin College, where Longfellow had attended. I remember from school days Longellow's "Evangeline a Tale of Acadie,"; "The Village Blacksmith" and "Paul Revere's Ride." He also wrote the sonnet, "The Cross of Snow" . . . ending with these lines:

> There is a mountain in the distant west
> That sun - defying in its deep ravines
> Displays a cross of snow upon its side,
> Such is the cross I wear upon my breast
> These eighteen years, through all the changing scenes,
> And seasons, changeless since the day she died.

This refers to the Mount of the Holy Cross near Leadville, Colorado . . . one of Augusta Pierce Tabor's favorite mountains.

****

The Armenians were early settlers in Maine and a very desirable people. Their homeland was the Armenian Republic and part of eastern Turkey. It is believed that Noah's Ark landed on Mount Ararat in Turkish Armenia after the Great Flood. Armenia has been invaded and conquered many times. Their people have scattered to many parts of the world. About A.D. 300, Armenia became the first nation to accept Christianity. During the 400's, they invented their own alphabet, translated the Bible, and established their own university.

Increasing numbers of foreigners were brought into Maine to work on the dam at Augusta, on the Kennebec River. At this time came the Irish. After the work on the dam was completed, they remained and were an asset to the town. They brought with them a special talent in art. They produced molds used to make columns. These were styled like Roman and Greek columns seen on stately buildings in the U.S. Tyke Molloy's family took part in this work of art.

Boothbay Harbor is one of the most popular areas down east of Portland. This is typical of the island area's calm, coastal waters. Kate, a Molloy daughter, and her friend, Esther Wuethrich , took me to Boothbay. Esther is the exchange student from Switzerland that I mentioned previously. The Molloys love her like one of their own family. As I rode along, enjoying the trip with the girls, I said, "How nice that you are taking me to Boothbay!" I hadn't thought of getting there, and it was a nice surprise. At Ocean Point we enjoyed the harbor and looking at the boats. Almost every town along the coast has at least a small fleet of fishing boats. The fishing industry and tourism are both important year-round business in Maine.

Maine's first industry was shipbuilding. I was reminded that the first ship built by the English colonists in America was launched on the Kennebec River in 1607.

I turned to Kate and asked, "Do you swim?"

Kate replied, "The water is too cold to swim very long."

I later learned that Maine has few sandy beaches, but this beautiful, rocky shore on the Atlantic Ocean is a sight to behold! I love to hear the splash of the water against the rocks. We walked out on the public float to take pictures.

I have school-day memories of a poem (whose author I cannot now remember) It is about the "rock-bound coast " of Maine . . . "the breaking waves dashed high on the stern and rock-bound coast . . . "

It was great to be with these school girls in Boothbay. It all ended on a happy note.

New England-style homes are beautiful. On drives around Hallowell and Augusta, I was impressed with these stately structures. They are all well-cared for and none were in need of paint. The shutters added to the charm of the houses. Mike pointed out a certain design of the houses, a regular pattern. However, each maintained its individuality. The front door entrance had two windows on each side. The second story had a window above the door, and again two windows on each side. There were, sometimes, variations that gave pleasing effects.

As we drove along on the tour of the homes, Mike continued, "Notice that front door with a semi-circular design above it? See the glass panels on each side of the door . . . the same height as the door itself. This more elaborate design indicates that the owners have more wealth and want to beautify their entrance in this way."

I was impressed with these New England homes and how this simple plan is followed . . . elaborate door design too.

I was fascinated at seeing the "Widow's Walk" constructed on the very top of some homes. This is an old tradition. This square-shaped, balcony-like structure is centrally located on the roof top to give a good view of the ocean. New England seafaring men had these built to give their wives a place from which to watch for returning ships. They some times did not see their husbands or sweethearts for long periods of time. They kept the watch for their return, and sometimes they never returned; hence, the name "The Widow's Walk!"

Widow's walk on the very top of the roof of these typical Maine homes. Wives watched from here for returning ships. Sometimes the ships never returned to port -- hence the name "widow's walk". Photo by Evelyn Furman, 1987.

A trip to Boothbay, Maine. Public float at Ocean Point. Left to right: Kate Molloy, Evelyn Furman and Esther Wuethrich, 1987.

Pronged tea strainer used by Augusta Tabor, now owned by Mrs. R. Parshall. Photo courtesy of Mrs. R. Parshall.

Mrs. Augusta L. Tabor

Signature of Augusta L. Tabor. Courtesy of the Library of the State Historical Society of Colorado Collection.

*Mt. Holy Cross, near Leadville, a Colorado -- a favorite spot of Augusta Tabor.
"There is a mountain in the distant West, that, sun-defying, in its deep
revines, displays a cross upon its side" . . . Longfellow.*

Evelyn Furman conducting tours of the Tabor Opera House. Photo by Edward L. Orovec, 1968.

Pictured are the two women who purchased, and restored, the famous Tabor Opera House in 1955 -- Florence A. Hollister, seated, and her daughter, Evelyn Furman.

On stage at the Tabor Opera House. Left to right: Florence A. Hollister, Theresa O'Brien, Bob Nelson, Gordon L. Hall and Caroline Bancroft. Gordon L. Hall, author of his recently published book, "The Two Lives Of Baby Doe", presented copies of the book to Florence A. Hollister and Theresa O'Brien. Formal ceremonies for this occasion were held April 29, 1962. A banquet, arranged by Mrs. Charles Gabarde, daughter of Mrs. Theresa O'Brien, followed the ceremony.

The Society of American Travel Writers presented its Phoenix Award to Evelyn Furman at a luncheon held at the Hyatt Regency Denver Hotel on May 15, 1990. Hal Haney presented the award to Evelyn Furman.

Guests at the Society of American Travel Writers luncheon honoring Evelyn Furman were Sharon Krueger, her daughter, on the right and Heather Walden, her granddaughter, left.

203

Evelyn Furman, displaying her award from the Society of American Travel Writers. Photo by Marie Smith, 1990.

Bibliography

History of the Arkansas Valley (Colorado), O.L. Baskin & Co. 1881, Chicago.

R.G. Dill: History of Lake County.

Tales of the Colorado Pioneers, Alice Polk Hill, Pierson and Gardner, 1884, Denver.

Leadville City Directories.

History of Augusta (Maine) by James W. North, Somersworth, N.H. New England History Press, 1981.

The Denver Post.

The Herald Democrat--Leadville.

Rocky Mountain News

Other sources of information were:

Denver Public Library, Western History Department, Augusta Tabor files.

State Historical Society of Colorado, Tabor collection in the Archives.

Vital records at Augusta, Maine, State Archives, Library and Museum.

Office of Register of Deeds, Augusta, Maine Courthouse.

Amon Carter Museum--Mazzulla collection.

Author's collection of old newspaper clippings, photographs, stories and interviews from old-time residents of Leadville.

Information for this book is chiefly from Philippe Laforgue's collection containing Augusta Tabor's own diary and scrapbooks, including newspaper articles, various documents, and photographs. Interview of Philippe Laforgue.

The Society of American Travel Writers presented its Phoenix award to Evelyn Furman.

FOR IMMEDIATE RELEASE   CONTACT: RICHARD GRANT
MAY 15, 1990   892-1112

TRAVEL WRITERS HONOR EVELYN FURMAN OF THE TABOR OPERA HOUSE

The Society of American Travel Writers, the largest organization of professional travel writers in the world, has presented its coveted Phoenix Award to Evelyn Furman for the outstanding work she had done in restoring and preserving the Tabor Opera House in Leadville, Colorado.

Furman was presented with the award at a special luncheon hosted by Colorado members of the Society at the Hyatt Regency Denver Hotel on May 15, 1990.

Built in 1879 at a cost of $78,000, the Tabor Opera House is one of the most historic structures in Colorado. John Philip Sousa conducted a band on its stage; Houdini disappeared from it; Florenz Ziegfeld's showgirls danced on it; Oscar Wilde spoke from it; and John L. Sullivan scored a knockout on it. The auditorium seated 880 guests in elegant Andrews patent opera chairs upholstered in scarlet plush, the same seats used in the best theatres on Broadway of its day.

Even more fascinating was its owner, Horace Tabor, a grocery store owner who grubstaked 2 prospectors to $60 and almost overnight became a millionaire when they discovered the famous Little Pittsburgh mine. Tabor divorced his Wife, Augusta, and married the beautiful Baby Doe in a lavish Washington D.C. ceremony that was attended by President Chester Arthur.

The Tabors spent millions in an extravagant lifestyle that included such things as a $15,000 robe made of gold and diamonds for the christening of their first daughter. Tabor also built an opera house in Denver and numerous other buildings when suddenly in the Crash of 1893, silver prices plummeted and he lost his entire fortune. When Horace died penniless five years later, he told his wife to "hang on to the Matchless" mine.

Baby Doe moved into an old cabin by the mine and for 40 years lived in total poverty, dressed in rags. When she was found frozen to death in 1935, she had just two dollars left of the one time eleven million dollar Tabor fortune.

Not much was left of Tabor's buildings either, all of them having been torn down except for the Leadville Opera House and that too was scheduled to be demolished in 1955 when Evelyn Furman stepped in and purchased it.

With her own money and her own hard work, Furman began the restoration of the theatre. No state or federal funds have ever been offered. Furman opens the Opera as a museum from Memorial Day to October, working as tour guide, historian, janitor and bookkeeper. She has written three histories of the building and the Tabors and is working on a fourth.

Her interest in the building began from a personal connection to the Tabors dating back to 1933, when as a girl of twenty she married a miner and lived in a mining shack for two years. Directly below her was an old woman living in terrible poverty. That woman was Baby Doe Tabor, once known as the "Silver Queen of the West."

As she stated in a magazine article, Furman says, "When I bought the opera house in 1955, everybody in town said that I was crazy. But I felt so strongly that this important relic of Western history deserved to be saved for future generations to enjoy."

Furman has accomplished this task, and in appreciation of her efforts, the Society of American Travel Writers presented her with the Phoenix Award.

The Phoenix Award was created in 1966 to honor individuals and organizations that through conservation, preservation and beautification further the appeal of the nation's travel destinations.

#   #   #   #

From the Court House Records in Augusta, Maine:

BUYER GRANTEE	SELLER GRANTOR	INST.	BOOK/PAGE	DATE
Yvette M. Sirois	Wilfred J. Sirois	Warranty	2271/150	Jan. 10-1980 / Jan 30-1980
Wilfred J. Sirois	Yvette M. Sirois	War	2223/128	July 16, 1979 / July 16, 1979
Yvette M. Sirois	Gerard J. Sirois	QC	2179/101	JAN 10, 1979 / JAN 19 1979
GERALD SIROIS + YVETTE SIROIS (JT)	HELEN SIROIS	WAR	1025/61	DEC 1, 1955 / DEC 6, 1955
OLIVA SIROIS	JULIAN H. MASON	WAR/COV MORT	674/78	8/15/1930 / AUG/19/1930
JULIAN H. MASON	MARY J. MASON	WAR	664/347	MAY, 31, 1929 / " " "
MARY J. MASON	AMOS E. CUNNINGHAM	WAR	664/286	MAY 13, 1929 / MAY 14, 1929
A. EVERETT CUNNINGHAM	ORRIN McALLISTER + CHARLES N. WARE QUARRY PRIVELEDGES	WAR/COV MORT	464/561	MAY 24, 1917 / " " "

209

GRANTEE	GRANTOR	INST	Book/Page	DATE
ORRIN O. McALLISTER CHARLES N. WARE	H.B. SAWYER	WAR/COV MORT	555/87	OCT 21, 1915 OCT 21, 1915
H.B. SAWYER	EMILINA DUFRESNE	WAR/COV TAXES	549/43	APR 22, 1915 " " "
EMILINA DUFRESNE	BENJAMIN W. COTE	WAR/COV MORT	534/166 (COP.)	JUNE 23, 1913 JUNE 24, 1913
{ Being the Homestead Lots of Said Augusta, Form of William B. Pierce Deceased				
BENJAMIN W. COTE	FRED O. BOYNTON	WAR	534/161 (COP)	JUNE 23, 1913 JUNE 24, 1913
FRE O. BOYNTON	RUTH E. PETERSON LILLA P. TAYLOR CHARLES A. MARSTON SUSIE E.M. BRICKETT NESTA P. RICKER HARRY P. FOLSOM MAXCY N. TABOR	WAR	474/104, 105, 106	OCT 17, 1906 NOV 7, 1906
WILLIAM B. PIERCE	WILLIAM L. WHEELER GEORGE W. PERKINS		111/133	APR 1, 1838 APR 1, 1838
FORCLOSED REDEEMED			147/203 148/65	

210

Know all men by these presents that we William L. Wheeler and George W. Perkins Jr. of Augusta county of Kennebec & State of Maine Traders in consideration of the sum of Six hundred dollars paid by William B. Pierce of the same Augusta County & state aforesaid the receipt whereof We do hereby acknowledge do hereby give grant bargain sell and convey unto the said Pierce his heirs and assigns forever a certain lot of land situated in said Augusta on the east side of Kennebec River being part of the south half of three hundred acres lot numbered thirty Eight on second range according to Nathan Winslows plan & bounded as follows viz beginning at a point in the westerly end of said lot which divides the north half from the south half thereof thence running east south east one mile to an eight rod rangeway thence south south west on said rangeway twenty five rods thence west north west one mile to rangeway between first & second ranges and thence northerly by said rangeway to the first bound being twenty five rods and containing fifty acres more or less To have and to hold the aforegranted and bargained premises with all the privileges and appurtenances thereof to the said Pierce his heirs and assigns to his use and benefit forever And We do covenant with the said Pierce his heirs and assigns that We are lawfully seized in fee of the premises that they are free of all incumbrances that We have good right to sell and convey the same unto the said Pierce and that we will warrant and defend the same to the said Pierce his heirs and assigns forever against the lawful claims and demands of all persons In witness whereof we the said William L. Wheeler & George W. Perkins Jr. have hereunto set our hands and seals this ninth day of April in the year of our Lord one thousand eight hundred and thirty eight

-Signed Sealed and delivered   William L. Wheeler (Seal)
in presence of Daniel Pike   Geo. W. Perkins Jr. (Seal)

Kennebec Ss April 9 a.d. 1838 Then the above named W. L. Wheeler & Geo. W. Perkins Jr. acknowledged this instrument by them subscribed to be their free act and deed before me Daniel Pike Justice of the Peace

Kennebec Ss Rec'd April 9 1838 Entered and compared with the original

by   J. C. Abbot   Register

Deed to the original homestead of William B. Pierce. Dated April, 1838.

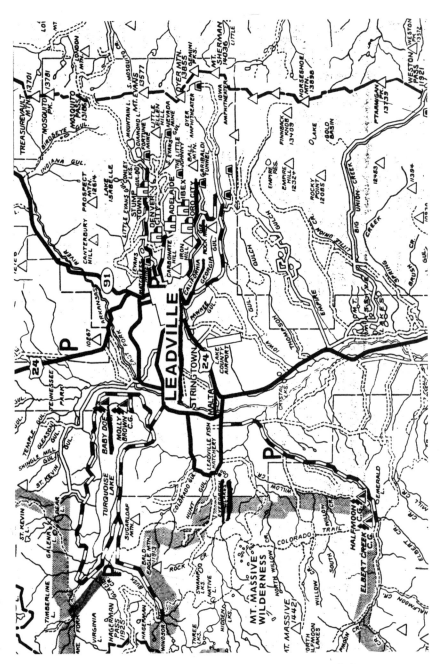

Leadville, California Gulch, Oro and Evergreen Lakes.

Leadville notables inducted into mining Hall of Fame

Three legendary mining figures with ties to Leadville were inducted into the National Mining Hall of Fame and the Fourth Induction Banquet Sept. 29 at the Marriott Hotel in Salt Lake City, Utah.

The trio is among 15 leaders of the American mining industry to be enshrined at the black-tie event.

They are Samuel Franklin Emmons (1841-1911), Robert Henderson (1907-1965) and Augusta Pierce Tabor (1833-1895).

Considered by many as "The First Lady of Leadville," Tabor probably conducted the first mining operation by a woman in Colorado, in the California Gulch district in

Ceremonies held last week in Utah

1860. She survived the silver crash of 1893 with a fortune. H.A.W. Tabor was honored in 1969. Their former home at 125 East 5th St. is a museum.

A prominent geologist for 30 years with the U.S. Geological Survey, Emmons authored many notable contributions to economic geology, including a monograph and atlas, "Geology and Mining Industry of Leadville," in 1886. Emmons also published the now-famous paper, "The Secondary Enrichment of Ore Deposits."

Under the dedicated leadership of Henderson, a mining engineer, the Climax Molybdenum Mine at Climax became a world-class model of underground mining innovation and productivity. The Amax Inc. Henderson Mine at Empire is named for him.

Engraved photographs and biographies of the inductees will be placed in the National Mining Hall of Fame and Museum.

Inductees include union organizer, former AMC president

At its Sept. 29 induction banquet, the National Mining Hall of Fame inducted Howard I. Young, who led the American Mining Congress as president (comparable to the current title of chairman) for 25 years, as well as 14 other legendary fig-

ures from mining's past.

The Fourth Annual Induction Banquet was held in Salt Lake City in conjunction with the AMC Mining Convention '91.

Besides serving as AMC's industry leader from 1934

until 1959, Young headed the American Zinc, Lead and Smelting Company, as well as serving as vice chairman of the War Production Board for minerals and metals during World War II.

The other 14 inductees were the following: Alfred Hulse Brooks (1871-1924), Chief Alaskan Geologist for USGS; Clinton H. Crane (1873-1958), president and chairman of St. Joseph Lead Company; Samuel Franklin Emmons (1841-1911) USGS geologist-in-charge of the Rocky Mountain Division; Donald Burton Gillies

(1873-1956), mining engineer and top executive with McKinney Steel and its subsequent parent, Republic Steel.

Also inducted were Robert Henderson (1907-1965), known for his leadership in molybdenum innovation and production; Ira Boyd Humphreys (1890-1976), inventor of the Humphreys Spiral Concentrator; Ira Beaman Joralemon (1884-1976), discoverer and developer of copper deposits throughout the Western Hemisphere; Robert P. Koenig (1904-1984), inventor and entrepreneur in coal and

copper; John L. Lewis (1890-1969), controversial president of United Mine Workers of America; James Wilson Marshall (1810-1885), discoverer of gold at Sutter's Mill; Ralph Baker Moore (1904-1969), pioneer in roof bolt manufacture; E.H. Snyder (1889-1967), metallurgist who developed a treatment of complex lead, zinc and silver ores; Augusta Louis Tabor (1833-1895), wife of mining magnate Horace, helped make Leadville a great silver camp; and Philip Wiseman (1885-1945), successful copper developer.

Augusta Tabor

Augusta Tabor inducted into the Mining Hall of Fame.